Stella Rowland

God In The Everyday

Roseward Books
OXFORD

Stella Rowland

GOD IN THE EVERYDAY

First published in 2006 by
ROSEWARD BOOKS
194a Upper Road, Kennington, Oxford OX1 5LR
(01865 736200)

ISBN 0-9552472-0-9 (10-digit ISBN)

ISBN 978-0-9552472-0-0 (13-digit ISBN)

Produced and printed by members of
THE GUILD OF MASTER CRAFTSMEN

Cover Design by RPM Print & Design
Book Design and Typesetting by Cecil Smith
Typeset in Century Old Style, Galliard and Shelley Allegro

Printed and bound in Great Britain by
RPM PRINT & DESIGN
2-3 Spur Road, Quarry Lane, Chichester, West Sussex PO19 8PR

Contents

Introduction

Stella Rowland, my mother, was a remarkable and talented woman. She had a deep personal faith which upheld her from childhood days until her death at 92. (She once told me that she had an experience of Jesus Christ when a very small child and that the assurance of Him as her Lord and Saviour had never left her.) Her faith held her through good times and bad – and there were many tough times and many when her own physical strength was low. I hadn't realised until after her death just how able she was to share her faith with others for it was then that I found, amongst her papers, the notes of talks she had given, mainly to women's meetings, in and around the towns and villages of the old North Berkshire. She never spoke much to me about the ministry she exercised in that way. But in reading her notes I realised just how remarkable she was, how imaginative, how knowledgeable of the Scriptures. Above all I became aware, as never before, of the reality of her relationship with God and of her daily walk with Jesus Christ. She also had what Kipling called "the common touch" – the ability to see and put into words the truths of God in ways that spoke to people not only out of her own depths but also out of theirs – and God's.

It was the discovery of those notes that led to this book. What she saw and had to say came from an awareness of Christ in the everyday which had become natural to her – almost second nature, as it were. She loved God with a great and enduring intensity and she found Him in relationships, in the world of tree and grass, cloud and flower, in worship both private and public, in great events and the events of every day, in music, and in the immensity and the immediacy of God Himself. Especially was it true that she found the beauty of God in the world He had made and was moved towards Him in her awareness of the world of nature.

She was born the eldest child of Cyril and Edith Moxon in 1912 in the village of Stewkley in Buckinghamshire. She spent the first 6 years of her life there, the latter half of that time with her beloved grandparents Joseph and Lucy Woodwards. The family were very committed Primitive Methodists, and in that church and Sunday School at Stewkley, Stella grew into a faith which led her whilst a child to that life-long relationship with God. That awareness, as I have indicated, never left her. She ever loved that village and that Church and it was always a delight for her when she and I (and occasionally my father) holidayed with my great-grandparents. (I can still recall waking early in the bedroom there, in that world so long ago, and hearing the milkman with his pony and trap coming down the quiet street. I can recall, yet, the smell of my great-grandmother's home-made bread and of my great-grandfather's little clay pipe. He was the gentlest man I ever knew.)

Stella rejoined her parents (and her two younger brothers, Bert and Joe) in 1918 when her father had left the Army and was working as a farm labourer near Didcot. The Primitive Methodist Church in that town became the spiritual home of the family. Stella taught herself to play the organ and by her very early 'teens was playing regularly at the church. After the union of the two Methodist Churches in Didcot she continued playing and, in all, served her Lord and her Church in this way for over 60 years. Her organ playing, her ability to lead the congregation in the great hymns of the faith, was inspirational. No-one who experienced evening worship in that church during the dark days of the second world war, the congregation swollen by soldiers and airmen, ATS girls and WAAFS from local bases, will ever forget the power of the praise which she led.

From the age of 6 or 7 she went to school at Long Wittenham, leaving at 14 and going into service. In 1931 she married my father, Albert Rowland. He worked in the family bakery at Upton and worked harder (and longer hours) than anyone I have ever known. (And even then, because the young couple were not well off, he used to cycle from Didcot to Upton every Sunday morning to clean shoes, light fires, chop wood and draw water for two elderly ladies. There was never any false pride about my father.) Mum and Dad's honeymoon was to go to the cinema at Didcot the evening of their wedding and to see a film starring Janet Gaynor. Dad was back at work the next day. His mother, for whom he had a great love, had died only 3 weeks previously and so the wedding day had much sadness.

I was born in 1933, their only child although they would have loved more. My parents were both glad and devoted servants of God through the Methodist Church. Stella was organist and also a Class Leader, a prime mover in "Women's Weekends", leader of the choir, and for many years President of the Women's Fellowship. At home she cooked and cleaned, tended her beloved garden, and was readily on hand to tend for the wider family when anyone was ill. She kept all the accounts for the bakery – and during, and especially after the war when bread rationing was introduced, that was a time consuming task.

Meanwhile my father worked 6 days a week from four in the morning until early evening. Three nights a week and every other Sunday evening he would be back in the bakery "setting the sponge" for the following day. At the same time he was a Methodist Local Preacher, often taking 10 or 12 services a Quarter in village chapels in the old Wantage and Wallingford Circuit. He had a little, old, Ford 8 and he cycled the 3 miles to Upton and back for work each day (often twice) in order to save his petrol allowance for preaching. I often went with him and can remember him picking up two or three other preachers to drop off at little chapels in the darkened villages. (Perhaps Jim Jeremy or Jimmy Morse or Godwyn Bradbury, perhaps my maternal grandfather Cyril Moxon or my great uncle Harry Wicks, one of them to be left at East or West Hendred or Childrey or Wantage and the last at the farthest western end of the Circuit, Challow Station, where the little Methodist congregation worshipped in a railway carriage by the side of the main Paddington – Bristol line. It was, of course, the saintly Jimmy Morse who, before Dad drove off would rest his hand on Dad's and pray first for "travelling mercies"). Dad was also a Society Steward at Didcot and, for many years, Trust Secretary. Truly our little family lived a life of service in home and work and Church.

In 1950 we moved to Upton where Mum and Dad had had their own house built on land owned by my grandfather Rowland. Sadly, in 1953 the family business had to close partly because my father's health was not good and the strenuous work of the bakery business was becoming too much. His brother Ernest who had also worked in the business had died suddenly some years before. However, at that time the advent of wrapped and sliced bread, produced by national firms was having an effect on sales. Hundreds, perhaps thousands, of small bakery firms were put out of business. At Upton, the bakery building itself was past its sell-by date and needed replacing at a cost beyond my father. Dad took what job he could find and after years as a craftsman in the baking trade became a messenger at AERE, Harwell. He did so without resentment or bitterness and I think he enjoyed his life there for much of the stress and strain had gone.

Dad had had only minimum formal education and was not an articulate man. (One of my most precious possessions is a letter written to me when he learned that I was offering for the Methodist ministry). But in the 1960s, and after the death of his father, he began to gain confidence and to flourish. Then he was diagnosed with Parkinson's disease. As the disease gradually took a stronger grip on him the large garden, the concern about the upkeep of the land attached, and the distance from church and shops, became an increasing worry for my parents. So in 1976 they sold their beloved home and moved back to Didcot. There my mother, with the help of some wonderful friends, cared for Dad as he became ever more unable. He never complained or railed against life or queried "Why me?" But he hated what was happening to him and the dignity which was lost as more and more had to be done for him. Stella and Bert celebrated their Golden Wedding in August 1981. A month later Dad died.

"You never get over it; you just get used to it" Mum said to me once when we were talking about Dad's illness and death. Get used to it she did, continuing her church work and her speaking ministry. Then she needed to move into warden controlled accommodation and, not long after, decided that she must sell her little car. (She had, years before, taken the driving test time after time after time before finally succeeding. She knew Dad would have to give up and was determined that they should still be "mobile.") Later she moved to Basingstoke, where Joan and I were then living, and valued very much the fellowship of the folk at Trinity Methodist Church and their kindness to her. By this time she had given up playing the organ and public speaking. She had suffered much illness in her life and now the effects of it all began to tell on her body – but never on her spirit. She spent the last year of her life in sheltered accommodation next door to us, suffered a stroke just after her 92nd birthday, and died on April 21st, 2004. She died in the assurance that she was "going home."

It had been in the late 1950s and then the 60s that Stella began her speaking ministry and it continued through the 70s and 80s. Some of the references in the talks published here reveal not only that she had been born into and grown up in a world much different from ours but also reflect a church and society now much changed. But I have left things as I found them, apart from a few very minor amendments, for this is the woman she was, this the way she saw and expressed things.

These talks of hers were meant to build up and encourage Christians – particularly the women in the meetings at which she spoke. I believe that in print they will still do those things. My mother's trust and confidence in God shine through everything. Her witness to God's gracious love and to Christ's promised presence kept her through everything –

good times and bad, pleasure and pain, gain and loss. In the midst of it all she praised God because she lived in the awareness of His faithful love – and answered it with her own.

I include also a poem written by my father, probably in the 1960s. For Dad, too, needs to receive his due worth. He and Mum upheld a loving marriage for 50 years and served God, each other and many more, with all their abilities. As a Methodist Local Preacher Dad struggled with his awareness of his own lack of education and personal inarticulacy. (His favourite hymn was "O, for a closer walk with God.") But he kept on, doggedly, in the awareness that he owed to God all that he could offer. In no part of his life did he ever give up. He was grit and determination personified. The poem was a surprise to me – but then during his lifetime I never realised *his* depths either.

My mother's Primitive Methodism (Dad came from the Wesleyan tradition) meant that she loved the great "gospel hymns" and found joy in Sankey and Moody, Torrey Alexander and Redemption Hymnal in addition to the great Methodist hymn book of 1933. Especially she treasured the PM hymnody with which she had grown up – a hymnody now almost largely forgotten. (Most of it far too evangelical, far too unsophisticated, for inclusion in *Hymns & Psalms* which is our church's present pale contribution to the Methodist tradition.) So I end with this: in the Primitive Methodist Sunday School Hymnal Supplement of 1912, there appears Annie Herbert's hymn :

"When the mists
have rolled in splendour."

It concludes with this verse :

We shall come with joy and gladness,
  We shall gather round the throne;
Face to face with those that love us,
  We shall know as we are known;
And the song of our redemption
  Shall resound through endless day,
When the shadows have departed
  And the mists have rolled away.

In that faith my parents lived and died. May this little book help others to do the same.

John Rowland
Spring, 2006

A Friend For The Lonely

(ST. LUKE 19)

Loneliness is a terrible thing. There are so many who feel imprisoned by it until and unless someone takes the trouble to get through to them. We thank God for organisations such as the Samaritans. Especially do we thank God for friends to whom we can turn. And perhaps it is when we feel most alone that we realise what a wonderful invention the telephone is. When we are anxious or distraught or truly "down in the dumps" what a blessing it is just to be able to ring and talk to someone.

In St. Luke's gospel, chapter 19, we read of Jesus meeting and offering His friendship to a man who was truly lonely. Zacchaeus was Jericho's tax collector. He was, thus, a collaborator with the hated Roman overlords, someone self-respecting people sought to avoid. No-one offered him a friendly hand.

When our Lord came to Jericho Zacchaeus was determined to see Him – from the safety of a tree! To his surprise Jesus stopped right beneath the tree, looked up and invited him to come down as quickly as he could. Before the day was over the friendship of Jesus had transformed the life of a lonely man. "Salvation" Jesus said "has come to this house." Onlookers were incredulous not only that Jesus spoke to the hated servant of Rome but that He went home with him. Zacchaeus, on the other hand, in his loneliness and longing, received the Lord with joy.

I am sure that at times Jesus knew what it was like to be lonely. (What must He have felt when His disciples fled Calvary?) Yet how cheering it is for us that just as Jesus took the initiative with Zacchaeus so He also takes it with us. No-one longs for the companionship of Christ without Him knowing it

This story is a wonderful example of the way in which Jesus befriends people. He restored to this man dignity and self respect and a new purpose. (As a result of his meeting with Jesus Zacchaeus gave half his goods to the poor and promised that if he had defrauded anyone he would restore it fourfold. Salvation had indeed come to his house!) The late, great Dr. Sangster said that Jesus sees double: seeing us not only as we are but as we might become by His grace. It is this confidence in us which holds us and leads us on. Jesus saw this lonely, this despised and hated man, not only as he was but also as he might be.

There is a lovely legend which has come down to us. In it, Zacchaeus is still living in the house by the Jericho road. Often he could be seen walking slowly to a tree and spending time in its shade. Sometimes he would rest his hand on it as if he were caressing it.

> "Why do you care for this old Sycamore tree?" he was asked. "Because" he would reply, "from the boughs of this old tree I first saw my Lord."

What a friend we have in Jesus – who befriends us by reaching out to us in our loneliness and despair, in our grief and suffering, in everything and everywhere. And by that reaching out, by that befriending, by calling our name and welcoming us, transforms our lives.

Amazing Grace

(Ephesians 2 vv 4-8)

We cannot comprehend the vastness of God's grace: it is higher than the hills, deeper than the deepest sea. We cannot fathom the depth, the height or the breadth of it. Grace is greater than all our sin. The reach of Grace is immeasurable for it is for all.

Grace liberates. By it we are set free from the chains that bind us – drugs, alcohol, pride, fear, jealousy, envy, strife, selfishness. In a sick world such as ours where the only answer is revival then we need the wonderful grace of God. Why do we allow all the things that cast us down and create chaos in our lives to enslave and imprison us, when the grace of God can set us free?

Grace pardons. We don't always find it easy to forgive or pardon someone who has done us an injury. But the grace of God is for all – no-one is beyond His redemption. He reaches out to the most defiled. His pardoning grace "so rich and free" was that which gave Saul of Tarsus the chance to change his life. It was the same grace that prompted Jesus to stop and talk to the woman of Samaria and offer her a new life, to give her a chance to become a new person. It was pardoning grace which said to the woman taken in adultery "I do not condemn you – now go and sin no more."

Grace forgives. "He was wounded for our transgressions", despised, rejected and forsaken – yet He could still pray

"Father forgive them,
they know not what they do."

Charles Wesley wrote (and we rejoice to sing) :

Plenteous He is in truth and grace;
He wills that all the fallen race
Should turn, repent, and live;
His pardoning grace for all is free;
Transgression, sin, iniquity,
He freely doth forgive.

This has always been my Church's great emphasis: all may live for Christ has died.

Grace is a free gift. How we love receiving a gift (especially as there seems little today that doesn't have a cost somewhere.) But God's grace is a free gift. God doesn't give and then charge a price. He gives, we receive. And He gives, according to the riches of His grace. God offers salvation and eternal life to all who believe on His Son Jesus Christ. What a joy it is to be able to sing from our experience what, again, Charles Wesley knew:

How shall I thank Thee for the grace
On me and all mankind bestowed?
Oh, that my every breath were praise!
Oh, that my heart were filled with God!
My heart would then with love overflow,
And all my life Thy glory show.

This free grace is for all. Not one is denied.

Grace is sufficient. We read in 2 Corinthians 12 v 9 how St. Paul had pleaded three times for the Lord to remove his "thorn in his flesh." God had said "No" and assured Paul that His grace was sufficient. How lovely to realise that although everything we ask for is not always granted He gives us the strength and courage to go on and by His grace to overcome.

As we move into each new day let us pray that we shall see the Spirit of God truly working in our midst and throughout the world, so that people will turn, hands outstretched and hearts open, to receive this freely given gift. What a turning back that would be to the God of such boundless grace!

Chosen

(St. John 15 v 16)

What a lovely feeling it is to be chosen to do some special thing. My memory goes back to school days when my friend Rachel was chosen to be the May Queen and I the Maid of Honour; or again when the same friend was chosen to play Alice in Alice in Wonderland and I was the Duchess.

In this lovely verse Jesus says to His disciples "I have chosen you." And, He says, that they are now to go and bring forth fruit and that their fruit should remain. What a privilege they had! But what of us? Well, out of this we can compile a list of the things for which we are chosen and to which we are called.

We are chosen for Joy. However hard the Christian way may be it is the way of joy. A gloomy Christian is a contradiction of what he or she believes. Yet so often we see too little joy on the face of Christians. What does Jesus say? "I have spoken these things to you that my joy might be in you and that your joy might be complete." What joy, then, should be ours in knowing that we are sinners saved by the grace of God!

We are chosen for Love. God commands that we love one another. Sometimes we live as if we were sent into the world to compete with one another or to dispute with each other. It is not much use asking people to love if we don't give it or show it. Jesus could say with all authority because He knew what love was: "Greater love hath no man than this that a man lay down his life for his friends." He did just that. And He has called us to be His friends – not servants or slaves. The slave does not know what his master is doing but "I have called you friends because I have made known to you everything that I heard from my Father." By making us friends God is no longer a distant stranger.

Jesus calls us to be His Partners. The slave could not be a partner but a friend can. To be a partner means we must share in the work and pull our weight. We are fellow workers with God.

We are chosen as Ambassadors. He says that He has chosen us to send us out. We were not chosen to live a life retired from the world but to represent Him in the world. We were first called to Him so that He could send us into the world. (And, of course, we know that we must continually come to God that we might be given the strength, wisdom and understanding that we need if we are to work for Him.)

He has chosen us to be Fruitbearers. We are to bear fruit that will remain, that will stand the test of time. The only way to spread Christianity is to be a Christian. We have to present a God who is so wonderful that others want to know Him. What sort of image do we portray? The fruit of the Spirit is love, joy, peace, long suffering, gentleness, goodness, faith, meekness and temperance, and this is the fruit we are to bear. We must try to live up to that. It isn't easy but to become more like Jesus is our aim so that others may see something of Him in us.

And then, ***Jesus chose us to be Members of the Family of God.*** And this so that "the Father might give you all that you ask in my name." This is one of the things about prayer that we don't always understand. We can – and must – take everything to God in prayer, but then we have to leave it to His perfect love and wisdom to know what is best for us.

Being chosen by God never means privilege or favour or preferential treatment. Rather it emphasises vocation: we are chosen and called to serve. His calling is to the privilege of sharing with Him His work of redemption. What we have is the honour of sharing with God His love for the world and being used of Him to lead others to Christ. This is what He calls His disciples to do and it applies to all who know Him as their Saviour.

Christ's Touch

(St. Mark 5 vv 21-34)

This woman in this story was one of a large crowd that gathered around Jesus. The people were fascinated by Him but there was more to it than that. He had been challenged publicly by Scribes and Pharisees but had answered them with skill and conviction. He spoke in a language that people could understand. So folk thronged to see and hear Him.

On this day there was this woman, weary and sick with her years of suffering. She had spent all she had in the hope of being healed. Why was it that she alone, out of all the crowd, should be the one who was noticed by Jesus? Because, in a way, there was a great deal of difference in the way she had come and the way those many others had surrounded Him. She came in her desperate need, and in that need and with whatever hope and faith she had she made living contact with Him. She alone was healed and cleansed and blessed by Him. There were many in the crowd that day with needs as great as hers, who heaved and pushed around her and might have been healed by Jesus had they had the faith of this one woman. She alone had that attitude towards Jesus which enabled Him to meet her need. He did a miracle for her alone, for she alone touched, believing. As St. Augustine says: Many thronged Him but one touched Him.

I suppose there has never been a time in history when Jesus has not had some measure of popularity. On His journeys around Galilee He drew large crowds. Today, on occasions and in various parts of the world, people crowd a Church – the Christmas Mass, the Easter Communion, the great Evangelistic efforts. But how many of us are really touching Jesus? Are we just one of the crowd or are we there because we want to put forth our hand and make a living contact?

The woman was drawn into the crowd that day because she felt that Jesus could meet her deepest need. She had been driven almost to despair in her illness and had tried every human help she could think of. For her, now, there was only God left to turn to and unless He could help her by a miracle there was no life left. She had heard of, and maybe seen something of, the wonderful things that Jesus was doing. "He must have a wonderful power and that power could heal me" she perhaps thought. "All I have to do is get near enough to touch Him. If I can just touch the hem of His garment, just make contact, then I may receive some of the power that flows out from Him." So on this day this woman came to Jesus: "If only I can push through the crowd and touch Him I shall be healed." What a faith! And once she had made up her mind to do this thing all that remained was to do it. Every other effort had come to nothing; all else had failed. This Jesus was her one hope so do it she must. Here was a woman who was desperate to be healed. Perhaps some of us were brought to that point of desperation before we could reach out to Jesus.

So she edged, nearer and nearer, to Jesus until at last she could just manage to touch the hem of His garment. But that touch was sufficient. She was healed and she felt the healing in her body. She did not have to go and plead with Jesus, tell Him who she was, prove her worth or anything like that. No, it was the merest touch that gave her healing.

How this story teaches us that we can come to Jesus just as we are! We don't have to be great thinkers or great achievers or great anything to come to Him. All this woman knew was this: if only I can touch Him. And that is what she did.

I am sure that her intention was quietly to creep away and keep this thing to herself. But Jesus was sensitive to that touch and turned and looked about Him and asked "Who touched me?" What a question! How would He know? The crowd was pressing around Him all the time, perhaps hundreds of people had touched Him in their desire to be near Him. But Jesus perceived that power had gone out of Him. All the others that touched Him did nothing to Him, but the simple touch of this woman drew power from within. Maybe the one thing that this woman did not want was a heart to heart talk with Jesus. She had found what she had come for. But she looked at Jesus and had to come forward and tell Him the whole truth. This was a full surrender, an outpouring of her heart. How many people today are like her? Are we wanting to enjoy the fellowship of the Church, to be in the crowd, to participate in the Sacraments, and yet afraid fully and wholly to surrender all to God? He doesn't want us to touch Him and leave it at that, but to come to Him, to learn more of His wonderful love.

After she had told Him all, He called her "Daughter," (her admittance into the family of Christ) "your faith has made you well." Then the blessing, "Go in peace – and be healed of thy disease." Here was a confirmation of her healing. This healing, this total change of life, can spring only from a face to face encounter with the Lord who constantly speaks to us through His word. Further: Jesus, thronged as He was by the crowds could make this woman's case a personal one. He is the one Mediator between God and mankind. He has the whole world to care for but He also cares for you and me. What a joy it is to know that however frail we are, however simple our prayers, if we reach out to touch Him His whole attention and concern will be ours.

Clay In God's Hands

(Jeremiah chapter 18 vv 1-10)

What a wonderful revelation this was for Jeremiah. To go to the potter's house and see him at work and then find that the word of God came to him. Isn't this typical of the way Jesus taught his disciples – by visual aids, familiar things, the natural world?

Genesis tells us that the Lord made Adam out of the dust but that he was made in the image of God (see Genesis 1 vv 26, 27). But, the story goes, Adam fell from grace and the image became marred. So we can think of the Lord as the Potter who knows just how we ought to be. The old hymn says :

> "Be still and let Him mould thee; I would Thy will obey.
> Thou art the skillful Potter and I the yielding clay.
> Mould me, O, mould me to Thy will,
> While in Thy hands I am lying still."

But after the moulding comes the testing. I am sure we are tested in many ways to see how firm in the faith we are. If we go back to the book of Job we shall see what happened to him. He was a good and wealthy man, a family man. He lost it all – children, cattle and, eventually, his health. If ever a man was afflicted it was Job. Yet he said "The Lord gave and the Lord hath taken away; blessed be the name of the Lord." Job's wife asked him why he didn't curse God and die. But Job would not let go: "He knoweth the way that I take; when He hath tried me, I shall come forth as gold." (Job 23 v 10). And, indeed, it was so, for God blessed Job and the latter end of his life was greater than the beginning. He came through his troubles. He had been in the firing but had stood the test. I wonder how we would stand up to so much. O, how the Lord blessed Job. God even gave him more daughters and sons and the daughters were the fairest in the land.

The potter looks for every small blemish – it takes the master craftsman to see the imperfections. Some folk seem to get more testing than others, but how wonderful if at the end we can say "Surely the Lord has been with me." He knows all about it. We are broken vessels and when broken vessels are mended they are often unsuitable for use. But God can take the most broken down life and make it completely whole. Sometimes it is the case that, as with the potter who is not very pleased with what he had made and starts again, a person is broken down altogether and remade so that God can really fill that life and make it beautiful. I remember a preacher, many years ago, saying that he lost everything, was brought down to rock bottom, but then he let God take over and he had never regretted it. He was given a new life. How many people there are who can testify to the same!

If we want to be used by God to serve Him we must be prepared to be put to the test. I trust that we shall be able to say, with Job, "He knoweth the way that I take; when He hath tried me, I shall come forth as gold." And with Isaiah (64 v 8): "But now, O Lord, Thou art our father; we are the clay, and Thou art our potter; and we are all the work of Thy hand." And say it with gladness for what God has made of us – and what He will yet do.

Doors

"Behold, I have set before you
an open door, which no one
is able to shut."

(Revelation 3 vv 7-13)

This was the text for my daily reading on the first day of the year. The more I think about it the more I think that doors are both interesting and wonderful. As I go around I find myself looking at people's doors. Many of them are very attractive; some are welcoming but others very forbidding.

The text says that God has set before us an open door. How welcome it is, when we ring the bell or knock, to have the door opened wide and the invitation "Come in." Often, however, it is different; the door is opened just a crack because the person behind it is fearful and has put a chain on. What a difference it makes when we know who it is and can swing the door open wide!

Doors in our homes have two purposes – to keep out and to let in. But we come back to our text which speaks of an open door that no-one will be able to shut. What a great promise this is. So let us look at some of the doors that are open to us.

The door of opportunity. You know it doesn't matter whether we are young or old, new things open up for us. And as we get older and unable to do the things which we did when we were young, God opens up new avenues for us. "I have set before you an open door." When our son was ill I met an elderly lady who, having asked me how he was, said that she couldn't offer to do anything very active "but I can pray and so many times during the day I lift him up in prayer." The door of prayer is ever open and how vital it is.

The door of welcome. There is a lovely illustration in the Second Book of Kings chapter 4: the Shunamite woman and her husband opened their door and offered Elisha a room whenever he came through that way. How good it must have been to have a place where he could rest and be quiet. There are times when we feel the need to go and talk to someone. What a relief at such times to find an open door and a welcome. The same welcome was given to Jesus in the home at Bethany. What a lot they would have missed if they had not opened their door to Him.

The door of prayer. There is a door both of opportunity and prayer that is ever open. Through prayer we can reach out to many people by bringing them to God. It can be a big adventure and, at the same time, bring us closer to God.

What about closed doors? In St. Matthew 6 v 6 our Lord is recorded as saying :

> "...when thou prayest, enter into thy closet, and when thou hast shut thy door, pray to thy Father which is in secret; and thy Father which seeth in secret shall reward thee openly."

In Acts 12 we have the lovely story of the return of Peter from prison. He makes his way to the home of Mary the mother of John Mark where behind closed doors they were praying for his release. Peter knocked on the door. Fearful who might be there, Rhoda opened it and saw him. I notice that they had been praying with the door shut – powerful prayer and an opening door saw the prayers answered.

So I feel that when Jesus said "enter into thy closet and close the door" (not to do as the Pharisees did, gabbling their prayers where they could be seen and heard) he pointed to the quietness of the room and that one-to-one relationship with the Father. In John 10 v 9 Jesus says that He is the door. Revelation chapter 3 has Him telling us that He stands at the door and knocks and that if any man hear His voice and open the door, He will come to them and be with them. Years ago we used to sing a hymn "Have you any room for Jesus" which contained the line "Fling your heart's door widely open, bid Him enter while you may." The people in the home of John Mark's mother were there with the door closed but with their hearts open wide to receive. It was the same with those who were waiting together at Pentecost.

It goes without saying, that the door to God is never closed to us – it is the ever open door which God, in His grace and love, has provided. He waits to receive and welcome us, indeed to welcome us home for we belong with Him. There is no chain on God's door. And then – O, then, to "fling our heart's door widely open" and to welcome Him with as much joy as He welcomes us.

Encouragement

(PHILIPPIANS 2 VV 1-12).

The first thing we think of when we hear the word "encouragement" is something akin to giving someone a pat on the back and saying "Well done, you are doing fine; keep it up." And it really is a good thing to do this from time to time for a little encouragement goes a long way. It can help someone regain confidence and find the strength to go on.

"Be ye encouragers of one another" says the apostle. How we need this in everyday life and how we need it in the Christian life. Too often do we meet together and paint gloomy pictures of the state of the world today when really we should be looking forward to great things with optimism and faith. The first Pentecost, when the Holy Spirit descended upon those disciples and friends, was such a wonderful time. They were so filled they could not contain themselves. That same Holy Spirit is still available and the same power that came upon the disciples is being given and is to be seen at work in the most unexpected places.

"Be of good cheer" the Master said to the disciples. The gospel of Jesus Christ is one of hopefulness, happiness and encouragement. In St. John's gospel we read "I, if I be lifted up will draw all men unto me." Are we holding Christ very high today? When we exalt Him we feel encouraged and our faith is restored, especially when we hear of people, young and old, responding to the exalted Jesus and giving themselves in the service of God. There is much good will and love to be set free in the world.

The words of encouragement the Lord gives to Joshua (Joshua chapter 1 vv 1-9) give to the new leader of the nation all he could need: "As I was with Moses so I will be with you…I will not fail you nor forsake you…do not be afraid…I will be with you." Joshua would need both physical and spiritual courage. The Lord promised to supply those needs – and He did.

Before He went to the cross Jesus spoke to the disciples about what would happen, but urged them not to be afraid. He gave them words of encouragement :

"Behold I send the promise of
my Father upon you…ye
will receive power from on high."

That power was truly given at Pentecost when the Spirit descended upon them and they became changed men and women.

God's word is unchanging. The same words spoken to Moses, to Joshua, to the disciples, apply to us today. God's Spirit is still being given. How encouraging that is for us! There are so many things in the Bible, God's word, that should lift us up when are feeling down. In our everyday life when we get worried about the future and how we shall manage we read in St. Matthew 6 v 25 that we are not to be anxious about tomorrow which will have its own worries. There is no need to add to the trouble each day brings! What could be more encouraging than that?

We not only need encouragement, we need to give it, so let us not withhold the word that will cheer someone else on. In his letter to the Ephesians St. Paul urges them to meet together and build each other up. We have a great God and a wonderful story to proclaim so let those who are strong encourage those who are weak.

I recall a little story about two shops both with a commodity that was not selling very well. One shop put it back in the store room and counted it as a write-off. The other made a big show in the shop window, presenting the commodity in a special way that was attractive. People looked, saw and bought until the shop was sold out. We have a wonderful gospel to proclaim, which will go on and on. Let us not be like the man who put the commodity away in a feeling of hopelessness. Let us endeavour to let people see that we have something to be joyful about so that they might want to try it for themselves. Let us be encouragers of one another in the assurance that God is with us.

Gifts

We all have a part to play in this strange but wonderful thing we call "life." We shall play it so much better if we use the gifts God has given us. Those gifts are varied. (What a good thing it is that we are not all gifted in the same way. How uninteresting that would be.) In Paul's first letter to the Corinthians, chapter 12, it says there are diversities of gifts but it is the same Spirit that gives them all. What a joy it is to know that God is such a giving God and that He has a place for every one of us in His purposes.

We have to learn how best to cultivate the gifts God has given us and use them for His glory. We do that by keeping our eyes upon Jesus. Often when things go wrong it is because we have taken our eyes off Him – we are more concerned with what someone else is doing. Poor old Martha was like this when she started to feel sorry for herself. We can sympathise with her but the truth is that she had taken her eyes off Jesus and was looking at Mary. Resentment broke the harmony of relationships. Then Jesus brought peace again by reminding her that the two sisters had different gifts. That is a reminder we all may need from time to time because it is so easy to look at what someone else can do, the gifts that someone else has, and to resent the fact that we don't have what they have. But we each have our own gifts and they are all to be used together so that God's work can be done as He wants it done. Your gifts and mine are all important to God and to His purposes.

There is a hymn which asks :

"What shall I render to my God for
all His mercies store? I'll take the gifts He has
bestowed and humbly ask for more."

Stella Rowland

How good it is if we can accept the gifts He gives to each of us with true and grateful hearts and praise Him not just for the blessings He and others bring to us but for those we may bring to others by exercising the gifts He has given. By doing so we shall be seeking to live in harmony with those around us and as we do that, as we use His gifts to us and welcome the gifts He has given to others, so we shall become so bound up with God and His great purpose that we shall become more like Him. And the more like Him we become the more loving and gracious we shall be, so that wherever He calls us to serve or in what capacity, we shall do it willingly and lovingly.

(Christmas) Greetings

It is getting close to Christmas and there are reminders of it all the time now with cards, wrapping paper, cake decorations, etc., on sale everywhere. We are thinking of sending greetings to friends who perhaps we haven't seen for a long time but whom we like to remember. Opening my bible to Romans 16 I read Paul's very personal greetings to many people who had meant a lot to him and to the Church.

He begins with Phoebe, commending her, calling her "our sister", a servant of the Church to whom he sends greetings. He asks them to welcome her in the Lord in a way worthy of the Saints and to give her any help she may need. Then he goes on: "for indeed she has been a helper of many and of myself also." What a marvellous greeting! Thanking her for work and her help to so many people. We know little about Phoebe but that greeting from Paul makes us realise what a wonderful person she was; a deeply dedicated woman living as friend and servant to others.

Then Paul greets Priscilla and Aquila "my fellow workers in Christ." They have, he says, risked their lives for Paul and it is not only the apostle but all the Churches of the Gentiles who are grateful to them. Just take a look at these two: Paul had been in Athens, then went to Corinth and there met Aquila, a Jew, who with his wife Priscilla had recently arrived from Italy. Paul went to see them and found they were tent-makers like himself so he stayed and worked with them. Each Sunday he preached in the Synagogues. When Paul left for Syria the couple went with him. Later they went on to Ephesus and there came into contact with Apollonius, a man with a great knowledge of the Scriptures and also a fervent speaker. Aquila and Priscilla invited him into their home and explained to him God's way in Christ (he having known only the way of John the Baptist.) These two opened their home for meetings of Christians and Paul sends his best wishes to them all.

Next come greetings to three other women whom Paul says worked hard for the Lord and then a greeting to a man named Rufus "and his mother and mine." What a lovely thought.

How blessed Paul was in having so many people sharing their homes and caring for him with such love. Notice how the theme of service to others runs through it all and how Paul emphasises their service to the Lord in so many ways. So he sends his appreciation to them all and he ends this letter with "Greet one another with a holy kiss."

With the Christmas season almost upon us we too have a chance to send greetings and thanks to those who have helped us in many ways during the past year. A word of thanks with our greeting can be an encouragement and we all need that from time to time.

I must mention one greeting from Jesus Himself. After the resurrection, when the disciples were met together, Jesus came and stood in the midst. His word of greeting was "Peace be with you." He came a second time when Thomas was with them and gave the same greeting. In St. Luke chapter 24 we read how He appeared to them again and greeted them in the same way. Those disciples with their troubled minds and hearts were still shocked at the cruel death of Jesus, still not understanding what was happening. But now His appearances and those comforting words "Peace be with you." Could we give or receive a better greeting?

Paul ends almost all his letters with greetings. I think that he, of all people, was an encourager of his fellow workers. He did not go around with his eyes and ears closed. Sincere, heartfelt greetings can mean so much to us. Christmas is a special time of the year when we can express what we feel. Who knows what a word of greeting can do. And let us remember: it isn't the length of greeting or the expense of a gift that lifts the spirits but the sincerity and love that prompts it. Such can speak volumes.

Guidance And Trust

(PSALM 32 AND ISAIAH 58 V 11.)

On a long journey to Penzance one year I was really grateful for our driver – keeping us on the (right) road which had been mapped out for him, and taking us where we wanted to go. But on another occasion, on a much shorter journey to Swanage I wasn't so happy: the driver deviated from the route that had been given us and ended up having to go back many miles to get back on the right road. The first followed the guidance he had been given, the second ignored it.

So we who love the Lord look to Him for guidance. In Psalm 32 v 8 we read :

> "I will instruct thee and teach thee in the way which thou shalt go: I will guide thee with mine eye."

And in Isaiah 58 v 11 :

> "the Lord shall guide thee continually, and satisfy thy soul in drought.......and thou shalt be like a watered garden, and like a spring of water, whose waters fail not."

What wonderful promises! The Lord will direct and lead us if we ask Him, and if we follow His directions carefully we shall not miss our way. But are we always willing to be led? Quite often we look to other things or people for guidance, instead of to God, and we can be led in the wrong direction. Some of you may have read the stories of Mildred Cable and Francisca French who, early in the twentieth century, went to China bearing the good news of the gospel. It is a wonderful story of hardship and fortitude. When they returned home and told their story to Christians in Britain they were asked why they had gone. They replied, simply, that it was guidance, "like being in receipt of sealed orders."

Gladys Aylward was also very sure that God was calling her to go to China, and being led by Him she went and did a power of good. We could mention many more but it would be wrong to think that only the great and famous are guided. We all need look to God for direction in our every day living.

In Proverbs 4 v 11 we read: "I have taught thee in the way of wisdom; I have led thee in right paths." We do need to seek God's wisdom for there are so many things that we do not understand, many questions that are beyond our knowledge. By asking Him to guide our thought we can begin to understand. But we need to be asking for guidance in the right way – in a way that honours God and His dealing with us – and we need to be asking for His leading, not simply confirmation of what we think or want or desire.

The story goes of a certain lady who was seeking guidance as to whether or not she should go on a Holy Land tour. She read in the brochure that the flight from London would be on a Boeing 747. Next morning she arose and when she looked at her clock it was 7.47 precisely. She took this as a sign from God that He wanted her to go. We may smile at that but I wonder if at times we don't tell ourselves that our own desires are His will for us? We may ask for guidance when what we really want deep down is God's approval for our own wishes. But if we seek His guidance we must be willing to be guided to His will, not ours. And His will for us may be quite different from what we want for ourselves.

There are times, I feel, when God speaks quite clearly to us and makes us know what He wants us to do or where He wants us to go. Many men and women have been quite sure that God has called them to minister in His name and they have been so sure that they have been prepared to give up good jobs, the comforts of home and many other things. All this under God's guidance to do His work. Sometimes it can be so clear. Yet I am sure that there are other times when God is speaking to us but we are not really listening.

Let us think on that verse from Psalm 32. Whatever we do we need instruction. In every day life we need to be told how to do things and we learn from someone who knows the right way. The Christian comes to God for guidance and it is wonderful to feel that once we accept His will for us then, as the Psalmist says, "I will guide thee with my eye." So the Lord is keeping His eyes upon us and likewise we need to keep our eyes fixed on Jesus our Shepherd. The shepherd walks in front of his sheep.

So our Lord goes before us, gently leading us on. This gives us great assurance, that He will never lead us into situations or difficulties that are impossible. He knows more than we know ourselves just how much we can bear or how far we can go. When we get into a train or bus or car we put our trust in the one who is in the driving seat. How much more should we put our trust in God and be willing to be led by Him. He says that He will guide us always in all wisdom, lead us along straight paths and keep His eye upon us.

As dear old Job says, "Thou knowest the way that I take." We can rejoice when we think of God being our guardian and it is comforting to know that He is also our guide, watching over and protecting us. If we are willing to be led He will lead us in His own ways.

There are people who are foolish enough to think they can climb a dangerous mountain without a guide. Valuable lives are lost that way. We know that life itself is full of pitfalls and dangers. How foolish we should be not to hold out our hand gladly and willingly and led God take it and lead us. We need His guidance not only for ourselves but for those who come to us with difficulties and problems. Having Him as our guardian should enable us to press on despite our doubts and fears; and having Him as our guide gives us great joy and confidence in our pilgrimage through life.

Stella Rowland

Into The New Year

After Christmas we shall be thinking of the Wise Men on their journey to find the Christ child. Their only guide was a star, but by following the star they eventually arrived at Bethlehem and the stable where the Christ child lay.

It comes to me that we are all travelling on and as each new year opens up before us it is a time for reflection. I think we must all, surely, look back and realise how wonderful God has been to us. We think back on good times and bad, but always God's guiding hand has been with us, showing us the way. It is said that it isn't too good to look back – and we think of Lot's wife for whom looking back was her downfall! But there are many things that we recall, some with joy, others with sorrow, yet as we step forward into the new year we realise that, as God has been with us in the past, so He will be with us in the future. In the hymn "One more step along the world I go"* we are reminded that we are travelling from the old things to the new and the hymn asks "Keep me travelling along with you." If we keep close to a dear Saviour we shall not miss our way.

The next verse of the same hymn says :

> "As I travel through the bad and good, keep me
> travelling the way I should; when I see no way
> to go You'll be telling me the way, I know."

What wonderful assurance that is. There are times when we do see no way to go – decisions we have to make that are not at all clear and we feel lost and alone. The only thing we can do is bring it to Jesus, leave it with Him and then let Him guide as He knows best.

*Sydney Carter; reproduced by permission of Stainer & Bell Ltd., London.

We know how Moses and Joshua felt when they were given the task of leading the children of Israel. But God told them to have no fear "for I will be with you." We have His wonderful promise that He will never leave or forsake us so we can be assured that He will not fail us.

The hymn goes on to ask for courage when the world is rough and to keep us loving though the world is tough. The verse ends with the repeated plea "Keep me travelling along with you." Surely we do need courage especially when we have to make a stand for what we know is right. We live in a world where there is much that is evil. When we look back at a year we may well be saddened that so much unhappiness was brought to so many. At the same time we are to be cheered by so many who are working continuously to bring light into a darkened world.

Not only, though, to keep going courageously but lovingly: "keep me loving." What a turning point it would be in any year if all the hating could be turned into loving. What a lovely world it would be. Where each one was concerned for the other. We are saddened because there is so much unhappiness and suffering. Where there is love, then hatred and greed and all else that destroys and harms will disappear.

I picked up a book that was given to my daughter-in-law as a present. It was written by a young woman who had been on the mission field. She and her husband had seen some of the wonderful work that was going on and found themselves saying "God can do it here." We do need faith and courage as we travel on. But to accept God's word, to believe His promises and to hold on to this is surely the key: that what He can do elsewhere and in other times and through other people, He can do here and now and through us. May we, as we go forward into a new year, learn to trust God even more than we have in the past. May we look forward with hope, and as we travel through life put our lives completely under God's guidance. He will not fail us. "As I was with Moses so I will be with you."

Keys

How important keys are! Many of us, when reaching the age of 21 (or 18 as it is now) were given a key to mark that special event. We felt that we were now seen as responsible people and so were trusted with a key.

Then there was our first home. What a wonderful feeling to be handed that key – what a sense of security to be able to lock the door and keep the world outside.

The car won't go, of course, without a key; many clocks need keys to wind them up. Lots of toys have to have a key (and what a pandemonium if the key is lost). Then there are cupboards and private boxes – we could go on and on. From this thought about keys come one or two others.

Keys are used to open and to close. We can turn the key in the lock and keep everyone out of the sanctity of our own domain, or we can unlock and invite people in to share with us. A key is a very powerful thing. If you have ever been shut out of your own home because you have lost the key you will know just how powerful. A key may be tiny – but it is so important.

There must be millions of keys in the world and people usually guard them with great care. When we look up a street of houses we know that there is a key to every door. When we look at life and the many challenges that we meet we can remember that those challenges are very much like doors: there is a key to each and every one. Sometimes we have a problem and we know the answer but cannot bring ourselves to open up and receive help that is there. Maybe it is pride that keeps us from turning the key and opening up the way. Maybe there is someone we haven't spoken to for a long time, perhaps some little thing happened, and now it needs that bit of courage to say a word that will open the door to friendship again.

Have you ever called at a house and the door has been opened just a little and you went away feeling unwanted? We can do that in our Christian life – let God in a little way and no farther. In St. Paul's Cathedral there is that lovely picture of Holman Hunt's with Jesus standing just outside a door. The key is on the inside. It is up to us to open up or keep the door closed. Jesus stands waiting.

How important it is that we don't keep things locked up within ourselves, creating great barriers. I expect that you, like me, meet up with people who have problems and will say something like "I am so tied up; I cannot be free." It is difficult to know what to say or do at such times. They hold the key but to be free all barriers must be removed. When the rich young man came to Jesus asking Him what he must do to have eternal life Jesus said "Go and sell all you have and give to the poor." The young man just walked away. He was rich and couldn't give it all up. So often there are little things that we want to keep back for ourselves and by doing so we prevent the Lord entering fully into our lives. We sing a hymn which says "All for Jesus" and another which says "Swing your heart's door widely open, let Him enter while you may." The great thing to remember is that our lives are in God's hands and He holds the key. How glad we can be for that. The more we open up and let Him in, the richer and fuller our lives will become.

Then, as Christians we are responsible to others. The various gifts God has given to us to share with others are not to be kept locked up within us. When we reach the age of consent it opens up a completely new era in our lives – we have to make our own decisions, we have the privilege of voting, we are at the age when we can make our own choices. As the years go by greater responsibilities will come our way. This is very like the Christian life. We are called to give out, and this is impossible unless we open up to God. If we want to grow as Christians we must let God take over entirely. This means letting Him right in, not just part of the way. Perhaps it means something more than that. Perhaps, by His grace we may come to that time and place where we simply hand the key of our life over to Him. What better, what safer, hands could ever hold it?

Kitchen Contentment

How important the kitchen is. For women of my generation it is the hub of the home, the place of preparation, our place of work. We have spent more time in the kitchen than any other room in the house. So we have wanted bright and convenient kitchens!

However, people who move around a great deal have to get used to different kitchens – some not as good as others. I read a book in which the wife of a Methodist Minister described some of the kitchens she had had. One had been L-shaped with one end of the room light and the other dark. She told of an occasion when a friend was with her and they were preparing fish. Going to the dark end of the kitchen to get vinegar she mistakenly brought ginger wine and the dish was spoiled. Dark corners can be so misleading.

The same can be said of some people – they seem to be two people and we are never quite sure of them. Of course, there may be something in our lives that we prefer to keep in the dark, but although we may be able to hide things from those around us nothing is hidden from God.

In another house this same Minister's wife had a lovely kitchen with a big window and lovely view. She found it a joy to work there as she looked out over the hills and at each season of the year there was something new to see. As she stood at the sink and looked out she could praise God for all His goodness. That anecdote reminded me of the life which is completely open to the Lord: knowing that there will be good and bad times but also knowing that the Lord is in every situation and can use it for His glory.

Another kitchen had a small window and all she could see was a tree in someone else's garden. It was so dreary she was despondent. But after a while the tree became something special. Buds on it reminded her that winter was passing and that Spring was around the corner. Then the buds would burst, the leaves would open up and it would be summer. She would watch the birds on the branches. Then there would be the lovely change of colour in the Autumn. The tree gave her so much joy. How different things can be when we look in the right way and accept the situation that we may be put in and use it to His glory. I am reminded of the lovely story of Dorcas in Acts chapter 9. She used the gift of needlework to the glory of God. She saw the poor widows and other folk who were in need and started to make clothing for them. She consecrated her needle to the Lord. Perhaps it was her only talent but she used it unsparingly for Him.

The kitchen is the place where we prepare the meals. At the moment Christmas is drawing near and much preparation is in hand as we try to get things right. How disappointed we are if the puddings or cakes don't turn out as they should. That is important, of course, so long as we don't get so busy that we forget we are doing this to celebrate the birth of our Lord – born with none of the glamour that befits a king but born in lowliness. As we make ready for that celebration may we make the very best of the gifts He has given us.

The woman looking through the one small window made the best of what she saw and from it found much joy. So God can take the smallest gift and use it for His glory. Love is the greatest gift. So as we work in our kitchens or, indeed, wherever we work, let us weave loving thoughts into all we do and ask for more of God's love in our lives, so that even in the most dreary situation we may see His hand at work. May the Christmas season be one of great joy and blessing to each of us and may the love that came down at Christmas fill our hearts with joy and peace.

Let The Beauty Of The Lord Be Upon You

(Psalm 90 vv 16,17)

When we see the word "beauty" what sort of picture does it bring before us? Maybe a landscape or a lovely picture, perhaps a building or a person. As I write, the cherry orchards are in bloom and are a sight to delight anyone. Recently I had to travel by coach to the Midlands and I don't think I have ever noticed so much colour. Daffodils and Forsythia were a radiant yellow. But there were many other colours and the scene would change as we passed fields with flocks of sheep, young lambs romping about. What a beautiful sight. That old saying is perfectly true: beauty is in the eye of the beholder. Often it takes the eye of a camera to bring out the full beauty because so often we just see without really looking. If we gave ourselves more time to stop and look we should be filled with wonder and amazement at the hidden beauty in a flower.

But we all know, too, that if we want to raise a tree or a plant to perfection we must watch for disease and at the onset treat it and keep a good watch. A relative of mine grows sweet peas for shows and the work that has to be put in, before they reach anything like perfection, is immense. He and his wife will be around the plants picking off the tendrils and watching for any threat.

Our text says "Let the beauty of our Lord God be upon us." Some folk go to a great deal of trouble to keep a good figure. They have to be consistent with diet etc., or the results will soon be noticed. We are urged to take care of our looks with many beauty aids. But what about spiritual beauty? We were made in the image of God so we should have a divine likeness. The same God manifested Himself to the world in His Son Jesus Christ whose life was altogether beautiful. That is how He would have us be. We cannot obtain perfection here, life is too short, but we can try to make the best of our lives. Gypsy Smith in one of his books says "Oh, that we may so display the beauty of Jesus as to influence all around us."

But to have this beauty we must have a pattern, a perfect pattern, and, praise God, we have one: our eyes are to be fixed on Jesus until His image becomes impressed. We try to copy His example and if we want spiritual beauty we must be like the woman who wants a good figure: constant in our habits. We must have rules.

We all know the rules of bible reading and prayer but there are other things also. We must have love for one another. For love is the golden chain of virtue and to it are joined lowliness and humility, meekness and patience. When we look at the perfection of Jesus there is no room for pride in ourselves. If we desire beauty of character we must cultivate the virtues. It is the inner beauty of a life lived in close contact with Jesus that shines out and is effective.

A story comes to mind of a young girl who was thought very plain but she made her life truly beautiful by visiting the sick and comforting those in sorrow. Wherever a door was opened she was there and she became known as the Angel of the Village. The greatest beauty of all, that of Jesus, shone through her.

I guess we have often heard it said that two people living together who love one another begin to look alike. Their lives are so wrapped up in each other that they become as one. I have seen this in people. This is what happens when we are daily in love with Jesus, when we talk intimately with Him, when we seek His presence more and more. We become more like Him and radiate His love and joy. Others will catch this joy from us. The closer we come to Him the more like Him we shall become.

This is what the Psalmist means by "Let the beauty of the Lord our God be upon us." There is an old gospel song which says "How can the lost know of Jesus, if they can't see Jesus in you?" It isn't that we are unimportant, that our personalities don't matter. How could we possibly think that, knowing how deeply God loves us and how much our Lord gave for us? It is, rather, that we have been called into the company of Jesus Himself and that in Him we find all that is good and true and beautiful, all that men and women were ever meant to be. We long for God's purposes to be fulfilled in us by our growing more and more like the One we follow. We long to be what God created us to be! We long to be in the likeness of Christ. We long for "the beauty of the Lord our God (to) be upon us" and about us and within us. Our daily prayer is to be found in that lovely line of Frances Jane van Alstyne's hymn :

"Draw me nearer, nearer nearer,
blessed Lord."

Looking And Seeing

Looking out of my windows I see the changing scene – Spring, Summer, Autumn, Winter – and I find great joy in it all. I love to look at the garden and the countryside, the flowers, the trees, the grass, the pattern of rain and sunlight. These I can delight in for ages. But other things I hardly notice. I am thinking now of how we look at things that really matter to us.

There is the rubbish pile and the beautiful flowering tree beyond. Looking at the tree we miss the rubbish. There are, in life, many ugly things that we hear and see, but there are many more beautiful things. It is the way in which we look which makes all the difference. What did our Lord say? "Why do you look at the speck in your brother's eye and pay no attention to the beam in your own." I like the little story about a woman who enjoyed looking out of her window to the house opposite. One day she realised she was not seeing very clearly so said to herself, "That woman needs to clean her windows." But on further inspection she discovered to her shame that it was her own windows that needed cleaning.

It behoves us to be very careful. Things are not always what they seem. It depends how we look. Perhaps we are looking at someone or a situation in the wrong way. We need to have clear sight, to keep the windows of our eyes clean so that we can see the best whenever and wherever we look. Jesus sees beyond the appearance of things. He sees the real potential for instance in Zacchaeus, despised by so many, but not by Jesus. The story of the Good Samaritan is of two who saw nothing but a bundle of rags and one who saw a human being in need and did all he could to help. All three looked at the same man but only one was looking closely and seeing the man as he really was.

As we draw near to Easter and our celebration of the

Resurrection it may be helpful to remember how some people saw the Lord. Herod in St. Luke (chapter 23 verses 6 – 8) had long wanted to see Jesus. He was hoping and looking for some sort of miracle and because he didn't get what he was looking for he sent Jesus back to Pilate. But in verse 12 it says that that day Herod and Pilate became friends where before they had been enemies. So you see, there was a miracle unseen by the two men. We see only what we want to see.

And what of Pilate? He certainly didn't see Jesus as a murderer. In fact, he told the crowd he could find no fault in the man before him. I have no doubt that Pilate could see something different about the man Jesus but did not, in the end, have the courage to go against the crowd. One thing stands out: Pilate had an inscription fastened to the cross: Jesus of Nazareth, King of the Jews. And when there were protests he insisted "What I have written, I have written." One wonders what Pilate really did see in the One who was brought before Him..

Of the two criminals crucified alongside Jesus one saw nothing except a fellow criminal of whom it was claimed that He had the power of God about Him. So he taunted Him: if you are the Christ then save yourself and us. Not once did he think of the wrong he had done or he might have seen Jesus as One who could forgive sin. On the other side of Jesus how different. Here was one who saw the Son of God alongside him, the Son who truly was king and begged Him "Remember me when you come into your Kingdom." Two men, both looking at Jesus and one seeing Him for who He was and receiving that promise, "Today you will be with me in Paradise."

In her book *Waiting on God* Simone Weil wrote that one of the principal truths of Christianity which goes almost unrecognised today is that the looking is what saves us. The thief looked unto Jesus and his soul was saved, he was forgiven.

And so to Easter day. John 20 tells us that early in the

morning when Mary, Peter and John went to the sepulchre it was empty. Peter and John went home but Mary stayed. She was looking for Jesus. She saw someone she thought was a gardener and begged him to tell her if he knew where the body of Jesus was laid. Then He spoke and she recognised her Lord. Jesus commissioned her to go and tell the disciples. I am sure her feet hardly touched the ground as she hurried back to tell them "I have seen the Lord." She had seen with her own eyes and heard His voice call her name.

In these stories not everyone saw the same thing. One thief saw Jesus for who He was – the other saw a reflection of himself. Mary began with seeing an empty tomb, then saw one whom she took to be the gardener, then she saw Jesus. We need to learn what it is to look beyond. We who seek to be followers of Jesus need to have the eyes of our spirits open to see His footsteps in the grass, His hand in the healing, to hear His voice in the speaking of our name. He walks the ways of our world and longs for us see the signs of His presence.

Looking Forward

God's promise to Joshua was "As I was with Moses so I will be with thee. I will not fail thee nor forsake thee. Be strong and of good courage. Be not afraid, neither be dismayed, for the Lord thy God is with thee wheresoever thou goest." (Joshua 1 verse 9).

I feel wonderfully cheered whenever I read these words. How marvellous God was to Moses. When He called him to lead the children of Israel Moses protested his inadequacy: he wasn't eloquent, he said, so how could he do this great thing? But when God asks that we do some special work for Him He will supply all that we need. God tells Moses that Aaron will speak for Him. God provided. And whenever Moses found himself in a difficult situation God never let him down. Never was there a prophet in Israel like Moses "Whom God knew face to face."

Now Joshua is to take over from Moses and these words are said to him. It was his task to lead a whole nation. He needed not only courage but trust and faith.

It's the same courage and trust that we need in every difficult passage of life. Whilst we admire physical courage it is the inner courage, the inner determination that counts most. How we need men and women who will not falter in upholding the right, standing courageously against indifference, apathy and opposition. We can see such courage in our Lord: in the wilderness, in Gethsemane, before Pilate, on Calvary. We often need similar endurance. We know that we cannot have it of ourselves but only as a gift from God. The disciples who had fled from the Cross found this as the Holy Spirit came upon them at Pentecost and they discovered the courage to declare themselves followers of Jesus. They no longer feared the opinion of others, they simply wanted to let everyone know of the love of God.

We too need courage, strength and faith as we journey through life and come into times and places where we are so unsure and even frightened. But by God's good grace, given freely, and His overwhelming love for us, we can have the confidence in Him that will enable us to go forward.

God promises Joshua to be with him wherever he goes. Yet what trust was still needed by Joshua! He had to learn that trust – and so do we. The more we trust God the more we realise how wonderfully true is His promise. But trusting does take some learning! If we are to progress in our spiritual life and if we are to find a true inner peace then we have to learn not only to sing but to live "trusting Thee, Lord Jesus." The late, great, Dr. Leslie Weatherhead wrote this prayer :

"Give us insight that we may see Your way.
Give us courage and patient endurance to tread it.
Give us faith to believe it will bring us out
where You desire we should be."

We walk on in that prayer in the strength and assurance of God's great promise.

Love In Action

Right through the ages, love has been the theme of song and story. The word is one we use to describe many things for there are different forms of love: the love of boy and girl; the love of music or art; the love of nature; and one of the best of all human loves, the love of mother for child.

Anyone who has a great love for anything or anybody cannot keep it to themselves. The love of boy and girl – however much they try to keep it to themselves – will soon be noticed by reason of the happiness that shows when they are in each other's company. A great lover of music, whether they be singer, player, conductor or listener, shows their love when they are enwrapped in it. The late Sir Malcolm Sargent when he was conducting, seemed to imbue not only the orchestra but also the audience with his love for music. The love of the painter will be seen in the picture he paints. And if you get talking to an old gardener or countryman, just watch his eyes light up as he talks about his flowers or plants, the trees or hedgerows. Then, Oh then, see the light of love in a mother's face as she nurses her child. When you love greatly it cannot be contained within.

So it is also that if we have the love of God in our hearts we cannot shut it in. There are, of course, times when we feel like keepings things to ourselves. There are also times when we are really lifted up and feel we want to remain in that experience for ever. Three disciples felt like that. They were privileged to go on to the Mount of Transfiguration and there they saw God in all His glory. They were so taken up with the wonder of it all that they wanted to remain. How lovely it would have been for them to stay in the atmosphere of that mountain top experience. But it could not be for there was work to be done amongst the people at the foot of the mountain and in the towns and villages round about. Stay they could not, but this mountain top experience would live with them for ever.

I suppose we all, at some time in our lives, have had some such experience. Maybe at our conversion. Maybe at some big meeting or in the quiet of our own home or that of a country lane, or alone with nature, or when by some means, some happening, some mood, we have been caught up in the love of God. We have felt His presence very near and we have wanted to stay. But as Samuel Greg put it in his hymn "While here we kneel upon the mount of prayer the plough lies waiting in the furrow there." However, such times are times of strengthening that will help us when we have our "down in the deep valley" days. This love of God is not just for any one particular person, any one sect or community, but for all mankind. The love of God is so vast that it embraces all and we are not doing the will of God if we try to keep it to ourselves.

Our Lord's new commandment was "Love one another, even as I have loved you." When we see the way in which Jesus loved we realise how very difficult it is to keep just a part of this commandment. It is so easy to love our friends (and, we hope, our families) but some people are not easy to love. However, Jesus' love went out to all, not just to disciples and followers, but to social outcasts, those who were spurned and rejected. His was a love that cared deeply for people. His love was compassionate, forgiving and sacrificial, love that gave of itself to the full. It was God's love in action.

As we read the Scriptures we find many instances of this. That love gave to the woman at the well the chance to make good; to the woman taken in adultery the chance to start again; to the woman who poured the precious ointment on our Lord's feet the chance to express her own love; to Peter the chance to regain self respect and value. This forgiving love pleaded forgiveness for those who crucified it.

We talk a great deal about a caring Church. If we are to be

true to that we must be outward as well as inward looking. Indeed, in this age when so many people seem to have lost the desire to be part of the Church there is much to be done outside it. We must be missionary minded, not only thinking of work overseas but that which is to be done in our own town or village or street. Maybe the house next door or maybe in our own home. Not every Christian woman has a Christian husband, or vice-versa. Not all Christian parents have families who think as they do. So often we are called to witness for Christ just where we are.

There was a group of women in our Lord's day who were known simply as those "who also served." It would have been nice to know more about them, their position in life, what they were like before they met Jesus, how they met Him. Only a few are named – Mary Magdalene, Joanna, and Susanna, for instance. But those unnamed women ministered in the name of Him who had done so much for them. Maybe the only way they could serve Christ was to care for the everyday needs of Him and His disciples. It is wonderful to think that while Jesus was ministering to others, these women were ministering to Him. This was their love in action. This is the love that is needed today. In a world where there is much hunger and poverty, much prejudice and suspicion, God is the only salvation and His love the one remedy. We all know our own capabilities, but whatever we are able to do, if we do it in His love we shall truly make a difference.

We ourselves may feel that what we do is just a drop in love's ocean. But if that drop was absent then the ocean would be that much less. And someone, somewhere, at some time, in some way would have gone on their way not knowing love that they might have known.

Loved And Loving

(1 John 4 vv 15-21)

The passage begins: "Whosoever shall confess that Jesus is the Son of God, God dwelleth in him and He in God." So we discover God's love for us in Jesus Christ. This is a love greater than we can comprehend. In Ephesians 3 v 15f we read that the love of God in Christ embraces the whole human family. That means the whole world, no matter what the colour of skin may be. He loves us all. There are so many things that keep people apart, but as children of God we are all part and parcel of His family and as such we are to live in harmony. We think of the breadth and length of His love and see it is never ending.

What does God ask of us? That we love one another. We don't always find that easy because real love comes from within and it isn't always easy to express what we feel. In St. Mark 12 v 28 we read that a scribe came to Jesus and asked Him which commandment was the greatest. The Lord answered that the first commandment was :

"You shall love the Lord your God with all your heart..."
and the second
"you shall love your neighbour as yourself."

If Jesus had stopped with God and not gone on to neighbour we should have been sure about our relationship with our Maker but not so clear about our relationship with our fellow men and women. There is, Jesus said, no commandment greater than these – no matter how much we debate.

In St. Luke 10 we read where a certain lawyer asked Jesus "Who is my neighbour". In response Jesus tells the story of the Good Samaritan in which He described a neighbour as anyone who sees need and seeks to meet it. When we think of all the suffering in the world that story comes close to our hearts. Perhaps we were not so concerned in the past as we are now. We have not loved our neighbours as much as ourselves. We think of the Priest and the Levite who passed by. It was a Samaritan who saw and cared and did something about putting God's love into action. It is only when we love enough to care that we are obeying God's commandment to love our neighbour as ourselves.

We know that God loves us not because we are good or worthy but because He cannot help but love. Not because of anything we say or do but simply because He is love. I remember, with a smile, that my younger brother, when a little boy, had been naughty and was reprimanded by Mum and Dad. But small as he was he knew that Jesus loved him and as they reprimanded him he sang "Yes, Jesus loves me." The love of God never ceases and loves us as we are.

The story is told of a missionary how, on her arrival in China many years ago, she was taken through the crowded streets. She felt a wave of revulsion sweep over her. "Oh, God" she thought, "how can I love these people? I cannot even begin unless you help me." Then a fresh sense of how much God loved her came into her whole being. She changed instantly and for the rest of her days she loved those people with God's love.

God doesn't look at the outward appearance but the whole being and if, like that missionary, we cannot love as we should then we reflect on just how much God loves us. The late Selwyn Hughes said that when we allow Christ to love us as only He can love, then love springs from a pure heart, a good conscience and a sincere faith. You don't have to force yourself to love. Love springs up when we surrender our whole being to Jesus Christ and allow Him to love in us and through us. Because God pours His love into our hearts we can give it out.

How about our love for God? Have we matured since His love first came into our lives? Do we still find it difficult to love some people? I'm sure we do. Love has to be that which is genuine and true and it finds its home in us as we think of God's word that just as He loves us so we are to love one another. Then we dwell on His love for us. Read 1 Corinthians 13 and then apply verses 4 – 8 to yourself. I did this and didn't think I came out of it very well. I'm not always patient and kind and I don't always want to bear things lovingly. But our aim is to keep our eyes fixed on the One who loves us so much that He gave His life for us. That same Lord is continually interceding for us for His love never fails or weakens.

The world is in need of God's love. It is up to us all, inasmuch as we have received the love of God, to shed it abroad. In 1 Thessalonians chapter 3 v 12 we read: "And the Lord make you to increase and abound in love one toward another, and toward all men, even as we do toward you." We pray that the love of God to us will overflow our lives into the lives of others.

So from our reading we learn that we discern God's love for us in Jesus Christ and we become loving people through discovering we are loved. Many people have little love for others because they themselves feel unloved. But as to God's love – well the old hymn tells us that that love "passeth knowledge, passeth telling and passeth praises." Oh, fill me, Saviour Jesus, with that love!

Martha

(ST. LUKE 10)

Martha was the elder sister and, perhaps, responsible, for the household. Being the eldest used to carry a great deal of responsibility (and perhaps still does) and those of us who have been in that situation can identify with Martha.

I think of visits of Jesus to this home in Bethany. In Luke 10 we read where He was passing through and, maybe unexpectedly, called in. How differently the two sisters reacted. Martha began at once to prepare a meal. You can almost imagine her saying, as she bustled about, "If we'd know you were coming we would have had everything ready." She would get the best china out and would be trying to do three or four jobs at once. No wonder she got het up and flustered. All the time she could hear little bits of conversation between Jesus and Mary and would be so afraid that she was missing something important that He had to tell them. She loved Him just as much as Mary did, but had a different way of showing it. She was so concerned to be a welcoming hostess.

Meanwhile, Mary was so glad to see the visitor that she just sat down at His feet and listened to Him. Sometimes, the best service we can render is just to sit still and listen. I remember an old farmer who said "I baint much of a talker but I can be a bit of a listener." However, the sight of Mary sitting quietly was too much for Martha who was tired and frustrated. She let it get the better of her. "Why should I have to do it all?" she asked, "Make Mary come and help me." Jesus understood what had happened (as He always understands everything.) He knew Martha was tired. So He said "Martha, you are anxious and troubled about many things. But what is really needful?"

What a lot we can learn from this. How our lives are cluttered up with things that don't need to be occupying us. How we fume and fret over things which don't matter a scrap in the long run. The folk who say to us "It will be the same in ten years time whether you do it or not so why worry" have a point. We are too busy, too organised in these days. We can be so busy doing the Lord's work, as Martha was, that we miss its purpose altogether. A house can be a showpiece instead of a home that is lived in. In the Church we can be so taken up with doctrine and detail that we can fail in the true mission of saving souls.

So we think of our Lord's reply to Martha – "one thing is needful." Spiritual values are the only ones that last. Like Mary we must take time to cultivate them no matter what else is left undone. We must sit at the Master's feet and let Him talk to us. Prayer is so often a pouring out of our own and other people's needs that we cannot hear His voice as we prattle on all the time doing all the talking and no listening.

The second time Jesus came to the home at Bethany was a time of sorrow. Lazarus was ill. The sisters had tried everything but all failed. They sent for Jesus but, inexplicably to them, He kept them waiting. (John 11 v 1f). Then came news that He was on His way. Martha could contain herself no longer. She rushed out of the house and down the road to meet Him. Would she upraid Him for His delay? No. She poured out the whole story of the last four days. Then we hear one of the great expressions of faith to be found in the gospels. "I know that even now whatsoever thou ask of God, God will give thee."

Faith knows no such word as "impossible." With God all things are possible. Lazarus was dead but Martha knew enough not to try and cope on her own. She would leave it all to Jesus. I think of those words "Man's extremity is God's opportunity." Sometimes He has to bring us to the point of desperation to make us cast our burden on Him. Martha's sorrow, hopeless as it seemed, was turned over to Jesus. It is the "I know" that made the difference. He was her advocate and promised her that if she truly believed that He was indeed the source of resurrection and life then she would see the glory of God.

Martha was to be reminded of that again, later, when Jesus told them to remove the stone from Lazarus's tomb. She protested that her brother had been dead four days and Jesus reminded her that He had said that if she believed she would see the glory of God. And see it she did. As we think again about her, with her fussing and fretting, we look at ourselves. We know that there are times when we get anxious and bothered and we try to carry our burdens on our own. Let's confess it: we can never succeed in our own strength, but with God all things are possible. So we must surrender to Him and trust in His wisdom and love. I think Martha had learnt that and I am lost in wonder at her. She so trusted the Lord and His relationship with the Father that she was prepared to leave it all to Him. May God bring us to the same mind and heart.

Mary

(ST. JOHN 11 & 12)

I believe it was Martha's sister Mary who, we are told in St. John 11 v 2, anointed the Lord with fragrant oil and wiped His feet with her hair. And in her we see three truths about love.

Firstly, we see love's extravagance. Mary took the most precious thing she possessed and spent it all on Jesus. There is a great lesson here. Love never stops to count the cost. Love gives its all. We women have to count the cost when we go out to do our shopping, but we can give of our love freely. Mary did not use the ointment sparingly but broke the whole jar over the feet of Christ.

Secondly, we see love's humility. In those days it was a sign of honour to anoint a person's head. In Psalm 23 we read "Thou anointest my head with oil." But Mary anointed the Lord's feet. I am sure she never dreamed that she was good enough to confer an honour upon Jesus. This that she did was humbly to show Jesus how great was her love.

Thirdly, we see love being shown without any qualms about what anyone else might think. Mary wiped Jesus' feet with her hair. In that society no respectable woman would ever appear in public with her hair flowing loose, but Mary was not conscious of what they thought. Her one desire was to show Jesus that her love for Him was sincere. We are told that the whole house was filled with the perfume. Any outpouring of love can have effects far beyond anything we ever dreamed. As we used to sing in Harriet Beecher Stowe's hymn :

As some rare perfume in a vase of clay
Pervades it with a fragrance not its own,
So, when Thou dwellest in a mortal soul,
All heaven's own sweetness seems around it thrown.

Two judgements were passed on Mary's impulsive act. Judas thought it a senseless extravagance and said so. But he saw things only in terms of money and market values. The Spikenard was very costly, worth more than the disciples could earn in a year. Judas was completely blind to the significance of the gift and when he said that the ointment could have been sold and the money given to the poor it wasn't that he cared for the poor but that in his heart he hated to see all that money thrown away on the feet of Jesus.

Jesus, however, understood and He praised Mary for her act. He understood her love which had prompted such extravagance, and so He turned and told the disciples "Leave her alone. She did this in preparation for my burial. The poor you will always have with you but you will not always have me." How cheering that must have been for Mary: that Jesus understood. It didn't matter what anyone else thought or said – her Master understood. How often we become concerned about what other people will think and so we stop ourselves from doing things which we know it would be right to do. But Mary ignored the crowd and what others might think or say. She saw only Jesus and poured out her love for Him.

Our Lord asks us to pour out our love. He would have us do things in His name, and in so doing we do far more than we ever know. How little did Mary know that 2000 years later this act of hers would be talked about and would be the means of inspiring others to offer their love to the service of the Master. It is so often the act of one person that will be the means of many being led to Christ. Wilfred Grenfell was a young medical student attracted to a Mission Hall by the singing. He heard the gospel message and the appeal made for those who wanted to dedicate their lives to Christ. Only one person responded – a very poorly clad boy who stood on his own. Grenfell felt ashamed. Why, he thought, the boy had more courage than I have. It was that boy's example that led Grenfell to go and stand beside him. We do not know what became of the boy but we do know that God used Wilfred Grenfell to go to Labrador and bring salvation and healing to many people.

We know that it was a little lad's lunch that fed the multitude. He gave all that he had. When we give our all to Jesus wonderful things happen. Our whole life has a new outlook. We learn the real meaning of prayer and the vast resources of God's power, because when we give our all then Christ can work in us. Martha showed her love by serving (and how wonderful it is to be able to work for God in that way). Mary poured out her love as, unstintingly, she broke the vase of precious ointment over the feet of Jesus. Isaac Watts had the truth of it:

> Love so amazing, so divine,
> Demands my soul, my life, my all.

That is what Mary knew. When we see afresh, or for the first time, the love of God in Jesus, we know it too. And we learn to give as Mary gave.

More About Friendship

Friendship with Jesus opens the way to a new relationship with others. Friends of Jesus become friends with one another because they all belong to what the New Testament calls "The Body of Christ." In the fellowship of Christ's friends we are all part of the family of God and His love should prevail. Here we are to feel for each other, to share each other's burdens and joys. This is exactly what our Lord does for us. He is a friend who understands us, who knows our innermost thoughts and feelings, who is at one with us in our joys and our sorrows.

The more we ponder on the friendship of Christ the more real He becomes and we realise that no matter where we are we need never be alone. What comfort it is as we learn to talk with Him more and more freely – and no restraints, because He is our friend. In the book of Proverbs we read about the "friend that sticketh closer than a brother." There is uncertainty about every human friendship but there is none about the friendship of God: it is sure and everlasting. I read somewhere about a writer who said that in his early Christian experience he was taught to stick to Christ, to hold on and not let go but that there was something he had found out since and that was, that Christ had stuck to him. The promise is that He will never forsake us and nor shall anyone nor anything be able to tear us from His hand.

How thankful we are then that Jesus, on His own initiative, comes close to make us His friends. How privileged that His friendship is not for a favoured few, nor for a limited time, nor dependent on us toeing a particular line or showing ourselves worthy of Him. "For all, for all, my Saviour died, for all my Lord was crucified" as Charles Wesley enables us to sing. In St. John's Gospel we read the words of Jesus that "Greater love hath no man than this that a man lay down his life for his friends." "And you are my friends" He says to us, "if you do as I command you." And what is His command? It is that we love one another. And isn't this the true joy of His, and anyone's friendship: to know that here is one who loves and cares?

Years ago we used to hear a song "You need friends." Of course we do. Life without them is loneliness and sorrow for we so much need those with whom we can share anything and everything and who will, in turn, share anything and everything with us. But as John Newton's hymn says :

"One there is above all others,
Well deserves the name of friend:
His is love beyond a brother's,
Costly, free, and knows no end:
They who once His kindness prove,
Find it everlasting love."

Thank God for Jesus our everlasting and never forsaking friend!

New Beginnings

Life is full of new beginnings. There are those that are joyful – the birth of new life, the child's first tooth or first words. Others bring apprehension – the first day at school or beginning a new job in a new place among new people. Then there is that very new beginning, marriage. How happily we enter into it, but what a lot of trust we need. Leaving the care of Mum and Dad, the familiar home; taking on a completely new set of responsibilities. Being adopted into a new family; taking a new name (and still answering to the old one for a considerable time, perhaps.)

And this is much like the Christian life when we accept Jesus as Lord. We leave behind the old life and take on the new. We have newly become members of a different family – God's family. The Scripture says that we are now "joint heirs with Christ". Isn't that wonderful?

But of course there are also new beginnings that are not as joyful and we may be not merely apprehensive but positively fearful. Retirement, for instance, can be good – or otherwise. Understanding is needed not only by ourselves but from those around us and especially those who share our lives most closely. The willingness to accept change and to work at it matter very much here. "Life is what we make it" becomes a deeply important truth at retirement.

The loss of a loved one and starting a new life on one's own is such a new beginning that it may well feel like an ending (which in one way, of course, it is.) For many of us the best we can say is that we never get over it, we just get used to living with it. And here, especially, our part in God's family can be, and should be, the biggest strength and help. So many of us can witness that the love and support of God's people have made all the difference. And then, how often have we heard people say, as I did only a day or two ago, that without the relationship with God that they have in prayer they wouldn't know how to cope.

Then, it comes to many of us that we have to leave the old home and move into a communal one. Something that we have never done before and which is such a very, very difficult step to take. "I dread the very thought of it" someone said to me. I suspect that most of us do. The thought of not being able to care for oneself any more, of being at the mercy of others. What a blow that can be to our sense of personal pride. A new beginning that betokens, again, an ending of something that was familiar and safe.

But in all this it is still true that every day is a new day. We may do the same tasks or it may be that we have to have them done for us. We may be active or we may be unable. But it is a new day and that is another new beginning and there will be fresh opportunities. And we have with us, in every time and place, the promise of our Lord that He will be at our side until journey's end. In 2 Corinthians 6 we hear St. Paul telling of so many trials and hardships through which he has come. Yet he speaks of himself and his companions as "sorrowful, yet always rejoicing, as poor, yet making many rich, as having nothing, and yet possessing all things." We, out of our own experience, join with the great apostle in witnessing to the same gracious God, and we praise Him for His promises and His presence.

Opening The Door For God

(Acts 12 vv 1-19)

Rhoda was a slave girl and her mistress was the mother of John Mark. Rhoda's duties included answering the door to callers and this meant that she came to know them quite well. She became a Christian and after the evening meal when the family and friends joined together for prayer she was with them.

What a lot we miss these days that we don't find time to gather the household together once in the day for worship and prayer. What a wonderful opportunity this could be, too, in places where people live in close proximity to each other – flats, bed-sits, residential homes. Simply to open the door and invite others in to share in praise and prayer. I read of one old lady, crippled with arthritis, living in a bed-sit in a large house that had been converted into individual apartments. She pinned a notice on her door to say she would be engaged in prayer every evening at 9 p.m. and anyone else was welcome to join her. "I'll give you a cup of tea if you bring your own cup" she added. From that simple witness there grew a rich fellowship. The landlady who told the story said that she used to find her tenants such a quarrelsome lot but now that had changed. "They are always trying to do kindnesses for one another" she said. Prayer changes things.

This particular night there was a prayer meeting at the home of John Mark and earnest prayer was made that God would deliver Peter from prison. As they were praying there was a knock at the door and Rhoda opened it to Peter. *While they were still on their knees the thing had been accomplished.* Before they had left their prayers he was at the door. They had not expected an answer so soon. Their faith was not equal to that. (Like the prayer meeting for rain where only one person brought an umbrella!) And I note this, especially:

Acts 12 v 13 says that "...as Peter knocked at the door of the gate, a girl named Rhoda came to answer." No waiting – even as he knocked the door was opened! What expectation of God the girl had!

We pray. But do we believe enough to go and open the door? We need the spirit of Rhoda who was ready to translate the prayers into action. If she had not opened the door this story would have had a different ending. We need to be ready to open the door and receive an answer. That night, they were praying with their doors locked and bolted, afraid of intruders. So often we may be like that – asking God for great things but not believing enough to be ready to open the door to Him.

But when we do open the door, why, we learn that God is at work today, answering prayers in wonderful ways. But we who ask must learn to trust and obey when God answers and to thank Him even when we don't get our answer, or one different from that which we looked for. So we need to make time not only to pray but to listen for God's answers; not only to pray but to be the means of our prayer being answered; not only to pray but to be prepared to do His will. There are times, for instance, when we are puzzled because we may be guided to do something quite different from what we had asked for and we need to remind ourselves that God knows what He is doing and what is best for us.

Prayer changes things; prayer changes people; prayer is the channel by which we contact God. But we shall not receive the true blessing unless we keep the door open to His possibilities.

Patience

Patience is a virtue not easily acquired and I do so admire those people who seem to have the patience of Job (as we say). But perhaps there is an impatient streak in all of us, born in us. I watch a tiny baby. It will soon start to cry when feeding time comes; it doesn't like waiting. Then, as it gets older, the child may go into little tantrums if it cannot have everything it wants. Watch that child, now older, in the weeks before Christmas or a birthday – counting the days because they can hardly wait for the presents that they will receive. Oh, yes, it is not easy to be patient.

In time of illness we get impatient if we cannot do the things we want to do. And so often we become impatient if we don't receive an immediate answer to some of our prayers. If only we could be more patient and wait upon the Lord, how much better it would be for us, for He knows better than we what is good for us. Again, there are times when we are discouraged by the pace of our advance – we do not seem to see any results for our labours and we wonder if we are doing anything to make this world a better place. Well, this is where we need patience to keep plodding on, never doubting the wisdom and love of God.

It was one of those mornings when everything seemed to be going wrong. Jane was late getting up, then the sweeper went wrong and it took ages to get it to go again. She wasn't feeling too well and had a nagging pain – not enough to make a fuss about, but too bad to forget. She wanted to do some baking but the oven was in a contrary mood and wouldn't get hot. Nothing was going right. Then, just as the oven started warming up and she had all the ingredients ready for her cakes the front door bell rang. She hoped it was only the postman or some such caller, but when she opened the door there stood

Liz, a friend from down the road. Jane knew that once her friend got in there would be no time for baking or anything else. But she felt for Liz who laboured on but seemed to achieve so little.

Liz apologised for calling, Jane sat her down in a comfortable chair and went to make a cup of tea. "I feel better already" said Liz, "I don't know but there's something about this house. What is it?" "I don't know" said Jane, "except you know you can always come here for a chat when something's happened and know that nothing will be repeated." "That's just it" said her friend, "nothing *has* happened. Nothing ever does. I wonder why I am here." "When you feel like that you need patience" said Jane. "Well, I've never found that easy" said Liz, "I've always wanted to see around the next corner. Not that I believe in reading the tea cups or such like, but I wish I could know just how things would turn out."

"But" asked Jane, "haven't you found out that if we are patient things do turn out right? Just think how frightened the disciples were when they were out in a storm on the lake and Jesus hadn't come. Remember, too, the feeding of the multitude and how the disciples were getting bothered about how they would feed the people. But Jesus had it within His hands. He knew what He was doing."

"Well" said Liz, "why did He not tell them that He was coming, then they would not have been so bothered." "Perhaps He did" said Jane, "and perhaps they didn't hear His voice above the noise of the storm. But in any case we don't tell God when to come or how. "Oh," replied her friend, "I wouldn't dare to do that. I wouldn't even dare to tell you. But I know you would come if I needed you." "Now look" said Jane, "you are putting more faith in me than in God. Isn't God more sure to come when you need Him than I am?"

"But He doesn't do anything. He doesn't appear to care. I pray and wait and wait and pray until I feel it is no use praying any more."

"Are you sure you are praying for the things that are best for you?"

"Well, these things are, I know they are" Liz replied. "I've prayed so much and waited so long. Hope makes the heart sick."

Jane realised she had not thought Liz capable of such deep feelings. "I wonder" she said "if hope deferred makes the Lord sick? Some of us are ready to do anything except wait. Then we complain that the Lord has forgotten us when all the time it is that we cannot wait patiently."

Then Jane had an idea. She asked her friend to go out into the garden with her, and she took her to a peach tree looking lovely in the sunlight and some ripening peaches hanging from it "You see that tree" said Jane; "I started that with a stone and year after year I have come out to look at it and it has been so slow growing that I felt it never would produce fruit. Again and again my hopes came to nothing. But this year – well, look at it now."

Liz hesitated for a moment – just a little doubtfully but at the same time just a little thoughtfully. "Yes, I see what you mean" she said , "all these years it's been growing whilst you just had to wait patiently. Now it's produced perfect fruit." She was quiet for a few moments. Then she said, "I shall have to go home and think about that."

We all get impatient at times and so often we want to run before God calls us to walk. We are not always prepared to wait His time and purpose. But we can be assured that He is in every situation. Jesus didn't hurry to that home at Bethany when the sisters sent for Him. He had a purpose and He knew that this was a time and place where the Father would be glorified and many who hadn't believed before would now believe. Just as growth was at work in the peach tree so, if we submit ourselves to God's will, He will work in our lives. We may feel at times as if nothing is happening, but God is working His purpose out and we must wait patiently for His time. The Psalmist (Ps. 37 v 7) has the way of it: "Rest in the Lord and wait patiently for Him."

Praise

There's a great deal to be said for praise – providing, of course, that it is genuine. We cannot get much more genuine than the Psalmist, and many Psalms (but 146 – 150 are particularly in my mind) are works of praise. They remind me how much it matters to offer this gift to God. And also that just a word or two of praise – "You did well," "I'm so grateful to you for all you have done" – can make such a difference to us.

Ephesians 5 v 19 asks us to give thanks and praise "singing and making melody" in our hearts. But we don't always need noise in order to do this. Praise can fill our hearts and minds when we are at our prayers or just being still in contemplation of some moment or scene of beauty. Psalm 150 speaks of praising with the loud, brass instruments and also with the softer strings and letting both glorify the Lord. How lovely it is when all are played together in complete harmony. Just as it is so good when we can join together in fellowship and praise God with one accord.

Perhaps the church at worship is most itself when, one with another, we offer thanks and praise to God. I sometimes think of this when I listen to a band or orchestra. Every instrument is needed within the whole, although some don't figure too prominently. Some instruments keep the tune going but the richness of harmony is added by the other parts. And here even the smallest, for instance the triangle, have their proper place (and how careful those players must be to keep their eyes on the conductor so that they don't miss their entrance! A second too early or too late would spoil the whole.)

Perhaps we are most truly ourselves as followers of Jesus when we – alone or in the fellowship of His people – are offering thanks and praise to the God of our salvation. And I think the picture of the band or orchestra speaks not only of congregational but also of personal and private praise. When the fellowship is united in praise it is making the best music of which it is capable. But I also think that when, in my own time of prayer, or when moved by some great beauty, when I am moved to praise of God then my whole being, in harmony with the Creator, is making the very best music.

The Psalmist longs :

> "that men would praise the Lord
> for His goodness and for His wonderful
> works to the children of men."

We have so much to praise Him for. For His great love to each of us; for His understanding of our needs, for the way He leads us day by day. If you have read about Billy Bray, the Cornish evangelist, you will know what a great man of praise he was. On one occasion he says "I lift up one foot and it says Praise the Lord, then I lift up the other and it says Hallelujah."

Our God is a great God and worthy to be praised in all ways and in all places, in jubilation and in contemplation, loudly or silently, in the great congregation or in solitary stillness. And, let it be said, praise does so much good for our souls as well. So it is good to give it where it is due, whether to God or to those to whom we owe our gratitude.

Promises

What a lot of promises we make as we go through life. I wonder how many of them we really keep? In baptism both parents and church make promises on behalf of the child and at marriage we promise to be true and faithful. Sadly those promises, and many others, are often broken. Time and again it is necessary to give a promise and the truth is not simply that it can be broken but that it can be broken so easily. The workman for instance, or the friend, who promises, faithfully, to come on a certain day but doesn't, causes us to lose some faith in them. A promise made by one person to another is a sacred thing.

We Methodists have, annually, a "Covenant Service" in which we make solemn promises. We pledge ourselves anew to God. We say that we are willing for Him to use us how and where He will; we tell Him we are ready to be put to "doing" or to "suffering" (i.e. allowing). But when it comes to it we often don't like what comes and sometimes feel like saying "Why me, Lord?" (Thank God He understands how we feel!) In the same service we are reminded of the promises of God which have never been broken. Every religious person knows that it is in His promises, not ours, that the richness and very foundation of faith is to be found.

The Old Testament has more promises than I can go through. But take that to Noah in Genesis 8 – a Covenant where God promises that He will never again flood the earth as long as the earth remains :

"Seed time and harvest,
cold and heat, summer and winter,
day and night, shall not cease."

Then God said that as a token of the Covenant He had made He would set His Rainbow in the heavens. What reassurance – not only a promise but a token, and each time we see the rainbow we are reminded.

Then in Genesis 17 there is God's Covenant with Abraham: Sarah shall have a child and you shall call him Isaac. Both Abraham and Sarah thought this impossible and laughed at the very thought. But in due time Sarah brought forth her son. God had kept His promise.

There are promises, too, that help us. God's promise to be with us wherever we go. What words of comfort those are. He will not fail us and He will equip us (as He did Joshua) for the tasks that are ahead.

In St. Matthew chapter 11 we have the lovely promise "Come unto me all ye that labour and I will give you rest." That "rest" means to be at peace and at harmony within. We may be doing nothing, we may be restless and uneasy; we could be busy – but we are bidden come to Him to find His gift of rest. So if God is our rest we can know this most truly when we are resting in Him. I think of an old hymn which speaks of resting in Jesus; and I think again of resting in the everlasting arms. How considerate Jesus was to His followers when He bade them come apart and rest awhile (St. Mark 6). That was a personal invitation which is still available today. The rest that Jesus offers is not so much rest from labour but a refreshment that will enable us to go on to the end no matter what befalls us. If we rest in His promises we shall be given the strength and courage to go on. So many are His promises to us that we may, indeed, rest ourselves and our cares upon Him for He cares for us.

Our Lord reminds us that our heavenly Father knows what we most need. So we can go on, trusting in His promises, knowing that nothing can take us out of His love and care.

Rest

Our Lord's invitation in St. Matthew 11 is "Come to Me, all you who labour and are heavy laden, and I will give you rest." When I think about resting it reminds me of a number of things – an easy chair, of sleep, of holidays which are a relaxation from the ordinary run of things.

How good it is to sink into an easy chair and put your feet up after a day's shopping. What bliss! This, and the other things that have come to mind, give us rest of our bodies and we can feel the benefit. But rest is not only a ceasing from our labours. It is also to be at peace and harmony within. How true it is that we can be sat very still doing nothing at all but inside there can be turmoil and NO peace. On the other hand, we can be very busy and yet have all the peace in the world because although we are busy we are resting in Jesus and leaning upon Him. That is real rest. Peace within God is our rest. I recall that lovely song from Elgar, often played at funeral services "O Rest in the Lord."

"Wait patiently for Him
and He will give thee
thy heart's desire.
Wait patiently for Him;
O, rest in the Lord."

Our Lord's invitation begins with the word "Come." I am sure that He knows just how much we all need physical rest. In St. Mark chapter 6 v 31 we read His invitation to His disciples and see how considerate He was for them – "Come apart and rest awhile." It was a personal invitation. He knew their need and, in His love and compassion for them, knowing they had laboured all day, bade them "Come and rest." Maybe

Jesus Himself longed for a little space of quiet in His sorrow for the death of John the Baptist.

When we go back to Matthew we have our Lord going on to invite them to take His yoke upon them, to learn of Him, and to find rest for their souls. I remember my Grandad carrying two buckets of water, the yoke across his shoulders. The yoke divided the burden and made it easier to bear. So when Jesus asks his disciples to take His yoke upon them it can only mean bearing something *with* Him. So when we come to Him with a heavy burden we can lay it down and take up a lighter one. His yoke is so easy, so considerate, that it is called rest.

How is this so? By the help that is given us in our load bearing; by the grace that strengthens us in our weakness; by the hope that cheers our weariness; and above all by His presence. We are not left to carry a burden alone for He shares it with us and with His wonderful invitation is also His promise of rest – that rest which we all so much desire.

One of the greatest examples of that perfect rest is in Jesus Himself (St. Matthew chapter 8). In the storm on the lake the disciples are filled with fear but our Lord is resting peacefully. When we are compassed about with troubles and trials, we do not need to get full of fear but to rest in the assurance that God is with us, that He will never fail us and that He is yoked to us to share, and thus lighten, our burden. O, what a blessing that is.

Roads

The Damascus Road – the road of Decision.
(ACTS CHAPTER 9)

Saul of Tarsus was travelling on this road when he met with an experience that changed his whole life. At the start of his journey his intentions were not good, but before he reached the end of it his life was turned upside down. God stopped him along that road. What a power for good he became!

We all tread this road. There comes a time in our lives when we have to accept or decline the call of God. Not everyone has the dynamic call that Saul had; for some it is a gradual growing nearer to God day by day. But whatever way it is, our lives are changed. Saul, having been confronted by the risen Christ, asked "Lord, what would you have me do?" His immediate recognition was that God was calling him, and when God told him what to do he went on not knowing what would befall him (for he was a well known persecutor of Christians.) But he went in faith and we each have to do that. It is not easy, but we have to trust in the One who has chosen us to serve Him as we travel through life. We are sometimes stopped in our tracks, as it were, and have to change our direction. I seem to remember the verse of an old hymn :

> Oh, it is hard to work for God,
> to rise and take our part
> Upon the battlefield of life and not,
> sometime, lose heart.

But if, like Saul, we can go forward in trust and obedience we can be assured that the way will be made clear before us.

The Jericho road – the road of Service.

(St. Luke 10. 25-37)

The parable of the Good Samaritan is probably the best known of all our Lord's stories. The Samaritan, on this road came across a man who had been mugged and left for dead. The Samaritan did all that he could – bound up the injured man's wounds, took him to an inn and paid all expenses for the man's stay until recovery. What more could he do? We are all called to serve and there are many ways in which we can do that. Like the story of the Samaritan we never know when and where our help is needed and we must keep our eyes open to see. Our Lord said that He came not to be ministered unto but to minister, to be the Servant of all. He never stopped to count the cost, not even when it meant death itself. Sometimes we are called to offer our service in places that are difficult, even painful or dangerous. We see a reflection of God's love in the Samaritan who gave freely and was prepared to give even more. This is the true love of God within, which leads us to the road of service, to love our neighbour and never shirk from duty when the need arises. When we become members of the family of God there is work to be done.

The Emmaus road – the road of Fellowship.

(St. Luke chapter 24)

This road reminds us of the glorious sense of peace and fellowship those two disciples experienced as they travelled back to their home after our Lord's crucifixion. Unknown to them it was Jesus who joined them and walked with them. We can have that same experience when we walk with the Lord. But how many times do we, like those two disciples, walk unconscious of God's presence, until He reveals Himself in some special way. The closer we walk with Him the clearer it will become. As Christians we need the fellowship of each other, the fellowship of the Church. As we journey through life we need the experience of the Emmaus road where those two disciples were given new life. "How our hearts burned within us as we walked and talked" they said, and new life was given them to go back to Jerusalem and tell the good news that they had seen the Lord. The Emmaus road, as well as the Damascus road, represents a way in which Jesus can come and transform our living and thinking and being. So we thank God for the different ways in which He makes Himself known to us and we pray "Open our eyes that we may see."

The Calvary road – the road of the Cross.

(St. Luke chapter 23)

Oh, this is no easy road. No-one likes carrying a cross. Yet we may be called to do just that. Some have heavy crosses to bear, others may not be so burdened. Our circumstances are subject to so many influences. We may find following Christ a comparatively easy and joyful road, things may go well and we find walking in His way a lovely thing. But if and when suffering comes or painful trials or loss or rejection or deep despair, why, then we may find ourselves saying :

"Lord, why me?"

In St. Luke chapter 23 verse 26 we read that "they laid hold of a certain man, Simon a Cyrenian, who was coming from the country, and on him they laid the cross that he might bear it after Jesus." What a privilege for that man just picked out of the crowd to bear something for Jesus. I am sure that burden was made light for Him. And when we find burdens getting too heavy for us Jesus says :

"Cast your burdens upon me for I care for you."

In His love He wants to help. What a difference it makes when someone lends a helping hand.

As we travel through life we may be asked to bear a cross that seems too heavy for us but the Lord will help us to carry it. We may even become stronger, for God can use these times in our lives to strengthen us, to give us a firmer faith and a greater understanding of His power and His infinite love for us.

Four roads but each one applicable to us all: the roads of decision, service, fellowship and the cross. And not one of them do we walk alone, thanks be to God.

Round The Vineyards

I know nothing of vineyards, but the bible does, speaking often about them. So let's walk through them in imagination.

The story of Naboth's vineyard in 1 Kings chapter 21 has a very pertinent message for us today. King Ahab coveted that vineyard. He wasn't satisfied with all his wealth but wanted something that didn't belong to him, thinking that that would make him happy. His wife Jezebel wrote letters in the king's name and sealed with the king's seal, the result of which was that two men bore false witness against Naboth and then saw him stoned to death. She told her husband to go and take possession of the vineyard. There he met Elijah who told him he had sold himself to work evil in the sight of the Lord.

All his craving for possessions, his wanting more and more of the world's good brought unhappiness on him and his family. The same spirit of wanting more and more, the same dissatisfaction, the same greed and covetousness causes great suffering to so many. Not least to the greedy and the dissatisfied themselves;

On the other hand, contentment, learning to live with what we have and are, can give great peace of mind, it can change us and how we see things. In Philippians 4 v 11 Paul puts it like this :

"Not that I speak in respect of want,
for I have learned in whatsoever state I am
therefore to be content."

Then there is the vineyard we find in St. Matthew's gospel, chapter 20. The owner of this vineyard went out to find workers and offered them a penny a day. During the day he hired four lots of workmen and at the end of the day they all received the same wages. Those who had worked all day were angry, they felt they should have received more. But the owner pointed out that they had agreed to work for a penny. He asked them whether he couldn't be generous if he chose to be. The parable suggests to me that all people are equally dear to God because He is a God of great compassion and generosity. The thief on the cross in those last moments of consciousness asked "Lord, remember me when you come into your Kingdom" and Jesus' answer was that that very day the thief would be with Him in Paradise. The last moment plea was heard and answered by a generous and loving Saviour.

We find the same thing again in the parable of the Prodigal Son. With what joy he was received back home. Yet how much the elder brother was jealous because he felt that he had been left out and that his younger brother was receiving more than he deserved. But the parable speaks again about God's generosity. "He that believeth on the Lord hath everlasting life." And this is for those who come late to know the Lord as much as for those who have been life-long followers. How generous!

And then, briefly, a word about the vineyard, the very first, which we find in Genesis chapter 9 verses 20 – 28. Noah planted a vineyard and made wine from the grapes and became drunk. Noah was a man who, we are told, "walked with God." He alone, with his family, was deemed worthy to survive the flood. They were God's chosen people who after the flood were pioneers of a new world. But the bible tells of both good and bad and the story of Noah does not leave out his fall from grace. He was a good man but he over indulged. To all of us that says:" watch your step!" It is so easy to slip. Paul warns us in 1 Corinthians 10 :

> "Let him that thinketh he standeth
> take heed lest he fall."

There is also, in the Old Testament, a story about a man who planted a vineyard on a very fertile hill and expected a good harvest. However, when the man went at harvest time, the vines had gone wild and the grapes sour. The man had great expectations but a big disappointment. What he had planted for, tended and longed for did not appear. All his expectant longings were dashed.

What does the Lord expect of us? What does He long for in us? St. Paul in Galatians chapter 5 tells us: the fruit of the Spirit is love, joy, peace, long suffering, gentleness, goodness, faith, meekness and temperance. We are part of God's vineyard and, as our Lord told us when He spoke of being the Vine, it is our privilege and responsibility to bear fruit to God's glory. He has planted His word in our hearts, He has given us His Son, He has tended and led us by His Spirit, forgiven our sins, picked us up when we were down and restored us when we were lost. Let it not be that His expectant longing for the fruit of His Spirit in us never comes to the fruition for which He longs.

Running From God

(JONAH)

When God asked Jonah to go to Nineveh Jonah had no desire to go. The city had fallen into evil ways and God wanted the people to repent. God called Jonah to go and preach to them.

But Nineveh was a Gentile city and Jonah was a Jew. So he decided to get as far from Nineveh as he could. He boarded a ship for Tarshish thinking he could get away from God and the responsibility that God wished to give him. But he learnt, as so many people have and, indeed, as we have, that you cannot get away from God. Psalm 139 reminds us of that so forcibly but so beautifully :

> "If I take the wings of the morning,
> and dwell in the uttermost parts of the sea,
> even there Your hand shall lead me
> and your right hand shall hold me."

God is always present.

Jonah was soon to learn this. A great storm blew up. Jonah was fast asleep but the crew were fearful and each of them cried out to their own gods. The Captain came to Jonah and urged him to call upon his God to save them. But then the crew cast lots to see who was responsible for this calamitous storm. The lot fell on Jonah who then had to tell them his story – who he was, why he was there and that he was running from his God. "I'm responsible" he said, "throw me overboard." But the sailors had mercy and in any case did not want to be responsible for a man's life, so they rowed harder. But this was to no avail and in the end they threw Jonah out of the ship and, we read, "they greatly feared the Lord."

I see a genuine response of faith in the Gentile seamen.

They were concerned for Jonah's welfare and did all they could to save his life although they knew he was responsible for their situation. They remind us of the many ways that people discover faith. As soon as they threw Jonah into the sea a great calm came down and the seamen feared God, offered a sacrifice to God and made vows to Him. God can use any situation for good. Jonah's presence in the ship was not useless. Through his presence the power of God had been revealed and these seamen had been changed. Moreover, Jonah realised that God had caught up with him. You cannot get away from God.

I note, too, the way Jonah prays when he finds himself in trouble. The story tells us that God had provided the large fish to swallow Jonah and it was inside the fish that Jonah realised what he had done. There he started to pray. So often when trouble comes our way, when we feel swallowed up by it, we can come to God with a depth of prayer because of our great need. Jonah, fearing that this was the end of him, poured his soul out to God. God heard the prayer and Jonah was spewed on to land where God spoke to him again. This time Jonah was ready to be obedient.

And now we find Jonah where God intended him to be in the first place – Nineveh. He was a reluctant prophet but a great success. The people listened to his preaching and heeded what he said. We are told that "they turned from their evil ways." Jonah was astonished. He could hardly believe what had happened. So we learn something here: we may feel inadequate if we are confronted by a seemingly hopeless task but the word of God is able to bring about changes that seem to us impossible. God saw the change in the people of Nineveh so forgave them and gave them another chance. Jonah, however, was not only astonished; he was angrily disappointed with God's attitude to the city. Perhaps he had expected to be proved right about the sinful people there and anticipated enjoying the judgment on them!

At the end of the story there is a little parable. Jonah becomes upset and obsessed with a plant that had sprung up to give him shade. The Lord had provided the plant but during the night it withered and died. Jonah was annoyed. The Lord said to him: "you are concerned about this plant although you did not tend it or make it grow. Yet you are not concerned over Nineveh, that great city. Should I not be concerned for the people there? Are they not more precious than this plant?" God showed compassion to the people for He was and is ever a loving and forgiving God. Jonah, in his heart, couldn't forgive.

Might it be that sometimes we are more eager for the judgment of God to fall than for repentance to bring forgiveness and new life? If that is the case then should we not be letting God speak to us and remind us – as He did Jonah – of the kind of God He is?

Stella Rowland

Spreading Our Wings

"As an eagle stirreth up her nest, fluttereth over her young, spreadeth abroad her wings, taketh them, beareth them on her wings; so the Lord alone did lead him…"

(DEUTERONOMY 32 v 11 & 12)

I read that the mother eagle builds her nest in some lofty place and lines it with feathers. After the young are hatched she gives them her complete attention, feeds them sufficient for each day. Nothing is too good for them. Then, after some weeks she changes her behaviour. She knows it is now time for her eaglets to leave the nest so she starts to pull it to pieces. She rips out the feathers that line it, breaks up the twigs that strengthen it and overturns this nice, comfortable home. The eaglets are frightened. Gently she nudges one of them to the edge and pushes it out into the air. The little bird falls like a stone, but before it hits the ground the mother sweeps underneath it and catches it on her wing, carrying it up into the sky. Then she gently tilts her body and now the little bird finds that it, too, has wings and it starts to fly.

So often, this is what God does to us: pushes us out of our comfortable nest, in order that we might spread our wings. How many of us, I wonder, have needed God to overturn our lives or change our circumstances. Maybe He has allowed us to be disappointed, maybe deprived, but in order that we might find ourselves. There is a lovely illustration of this in John 16. Jesus announces to His disciples that He is going away for good. Such news must have hit them like a bomb. What would they do without Him? They had left home, and family and work to be with Jesus. He was their strength. But in John 16 verse 7 He says that His going is for their good.

> "If I do not depart the helper
> will not come to you."

It was time for them to stand on their own feet.

The disciples must have felt very fearful at the thought of life without their leader. What they didn't know then, but would find out later at Pentecost, was that the Holy Spirit had given them unlimited resources. They would be able to do what they had thought they could never do. By taking away His bodily presence He would give them His spiritual presence that they might spread their wings.

The eagle can soar higher than any other bird and does so without flapping its wings. It has a knowledge of the air currents and waits for the right moment. Then it ascends without great effort. How much we can learn from that. We use up so much energy when we get in a flap, as it were. When too many things crowd into our lives how we react can make such a difference. We can panic and flap or react with confidence and courage. Isaiah: says :

> "They that wait upon the Lord shall mount up with wings as eagles. They shall run and not be weary, they shall walk and not faint."

Note the words "mount up." The behaviour of the eagle helps us to understand that verse so much better. By waiting for the right current the eagle is able to soar, reserving energy it would otherwise use. Those that wait are those that mount up.

So God sometimes moves us out of our comfortable lives. Many folk would never have made the best of themselves had they not been pushed along and thus found they could do what they didn't think was possible. A whole new world opens up. And so in our spiritual life, we can get in a rut and need a little push as it were. We can get too comfortable so that we are suspicious of change, yet so often we need to accept that we can move forward. And we know that if we do it in the name of the Lord and for His sake he will lift us up. If we wait for the Lord He will show us His perfect will. We may have to wait for a while, as the eagle waits for the right current of air, but having waited the journey will be easier. When our lives seem overturned by troubles and trials that come our way, let us not panic but wait, and we shall find that God will give us the ability to soar above all that assails us.

That Lovely Fragrance

There is a beautiful phrase in Paul's Second letter to Corinth, chapter 2, where he says that "we are to God the fragrance of Christ..." And I think what a delightful thing a sweet scent is. Each smell is different. A flower is identified by its perfume. Violets are tiny but they have a strong scent and we know they are there before we see them. Roses, Lily of the Valley, Carnations – they are all identified by their perfume. We recognise things and places (and sometimes people) by the aroma. Herbs each have their own scent – mint, sage, rosemary, etc. We go into a room where people have been smoking and we have no difficulty in identifying the smell.

As Christians we hope to be identified by the very way we live our lives, by our behaviour, our activities and deeds. We can all think about people who have passed on but whose lives were lived in such closeness to Christ that they yet live – the aroma of Christ which was about them still lingers. We have that lovely story about Mary who anointed the feet of Christ with the most precious and costly ointment. We are told that the fragrance filled the house. I believe that any good deed that is done leaves behind a pleasing aroma that lingers. I am sure that all Christian people would like to feel that something good about them would live on, that they might be remembered as a "sweet smelling fragrance."

St. Paul asks who is sufficient for these things. Well, we are by the grace of God. In Romans 16 he speaks of Phoebe whose particular service he does not tell us but for whom he does expresses his gratitude. What she did was so special that Paul commended her to the Church and asked that they assist her in whatever she asked of them. What a wonderful thing to have been "a helper of many." It isn't always by doing the great things in life that matters, being in the limelight for instance, so much as serving God – perhaps quite quietly in the day to day things. The violet and the lily of the valley are small and quite insignificant yet they diffuse a lovely scent that will fill the place where they are.

In our everyday lives we can, by God's good grace, show forth His love and we too can be as a sweet aroma diffusing sweetness and love wherever we are. It was a servant girl who wrote these lines :

Lord of all pots and pans and things
Since I've no time to be
A saint by doing lovely things
Or watching late with Thee,
Or dreaming in the dawn light
Or storming heaven's gate,
Make me a saint by getting meals
And washing up the plates.

Although I must have Martha's hands
I have a Mary mind
And when I black the shoes
Thy sandals, Lord, I find.
I think of how they trod the earth
What time I scrub the floor.
Accept this meditation Lord,
I haven't time for more.

Warm all the kitchen with Thy love
And light it with Thy peace;
Forgive me all the worrying
And make all grumbling cease.
Thou who didst love to give man food
In room or by the sea,
Accept this service that I do –
I do it unto Thee.

Those words call to my mind a saying that my beloved husband often used :

> "I shall pass this way but once.
> Therefore, if there be any good
> that I can do, let me do it now; for
> I shall not pass this way again."

What a fragrance we shall leave in any place and time if we do whatever we have to do, however menial, in the name, and for the glory, of the Lord.

The Armour Of God

(EPHESIANS 6 VV 10-20)

We need all the protection we can get in our living as Christians. So, just as fighting men of old went into battle armoured against the enemy we too are to protect ourselves – but with the armour of God. This passage from Ephesians tells us the armour we need.

First of all truth around our waist, holding everything else in place. Satan will put into our heads all sorts of things against the truth of God's word (the word which Satan hates.) But that word stands secure. Psalm 91 verse 4 tells us that :

> "his truth shall be thy shield and buckler.

Then, the breastplate of righteousness. The breastplate covers the heart and how we do need to be protected in this most vulnerable part of our being. How often we hear people say they have "lost heart" when things haven't gone right. People so often feel unworthy and helpless and at such times it is easy to fall out of the fight. But it is at just those times we need to recognise that however frail we may be, however prone to failure, however inadequate, our only confidence and trust must be in Jesus Christ. He alone is our protection and our defence so we need to wear the breastplate of righteousness – right living.

Thirdly, shoes that will speed us on as we preach the gospel. Oh, how important shoes are. If we walk much we need well shod feet. In Romans 10 v 15 we read :

> "how beautiful are
> the feet of them that preach
> the gospel of peace."

Every Christian is a witness for that gospel and so needs to be clad ready to give an answer for the hope that is in him or her. How nice and comforting it is to take off our shoes and put on slippers, but I feel that sometimes we tend to do that as Christians – we want things made easy for us. But we are to be at the ready.

Fourth, then, the shield of faith. Held out in front of the soldier's body it deflected the arrows and lunges of the opponent. God has given us faith. Some people have no doubts at all, others are different. The question is: will our faith stand in our stead in all circumstances? Do we hold on fast to God's promises? Our reading urges us to take the shield of faith to quench "the fiery darts" fired at us. How much we need to have that faith! In 2 Corinthians 5 v 7 it says we walk by faith not by sight. It is easy to believe in something we can see, but to have faith in what isn't visible isn't so easy. So we need to pray for stronger faith – and use what we have.

Fifth, the helmet of salvation as protection for our minds. The mind can create despair or happiness. We need food for thought to keep our minds healthy. Our own spiritual condition depends on the word of God and an ever deepening prayer life. Jesus' reply to the tempter was that Man shall not live by bread alone but by every word that proceeds out of the mouth of God. So we have God's precious word, and the Sword of the Spirit is the Word of God. When Satan tempts us – use the name of Jesus.

We need the whole armour but that is no avail unless wearing that armour is a living, breathing, Christian who knows the value and power of prayer. Our passage goes on to speak of praying always in the Spirit and watching for the saints. Communion with the Lord at all times, in all places. All forms of prayer and watching. Oh, what a great power would flow into the Church if Christians could truly believe that the power of God can break down any barriers; that we are one family in Christ Jesus and that by His love and grace we can build each other up. Oh, that we might lift high the cross of Christ and stand fast as one people. An army does not go unprepared into battle, but is trained and equipped to meet the danger. In His word we have all the protection and all the weapons necessary to enable us to stand fast. But it is in His armour that we must stand, nothing less will do. Truth and righteousness are to be our standards; the gospel witness our privileged task; faith in Christ our power and protection; salvation our assurance. With these gifts of God we can face, and overcome, any Goliaths!

The Christian's Walk

"I, therefore, the prisoner of the Lord,
beseech you that ye walk worthy of the vocation
wherewith ye are called.

(EPHESIANS 4 V 1; SEE ALSO COLOSSIANS 1 VV 9,10).

Whenever we join an organisation we should accept to live by its rules. Some people, however, may join just to belong, not bothering about the requirements of belonging. This can happen to Christians and is a very real spiritual danger: belonging in name only. Again, there is the danger of withdrawal, maybe through failure or disenchantment. It seems we can never attain the high standards set before us: we feel ineffective and we are tempted to give up the struggle. But to "walk worthy" compels us to face the questions of Christian living. Colossians 2 v 6 says :

"As ye have therefore received
Christ Jesus the Lord, so walk ye in Him."

We remember, with gratitude, that God does not ask the impossible of us: "All things are possible through Christ who strengthens me" says St. Paul.

So we are to *walk in love* (walking as Christ walked). Surely this is the essence of Christian living? God is love and the closer we live to Christ the more filled with love we shall become. We are told that there are many gifts which we are open to receive but that the greatest is love. Ephesians 5 v 2 urges us "...walk in love, as Christ also hath loved us." A happy home is where love is, a united family; a Church that is a welcoming and alive is one where those who make up the fellowship are open to God's love, who meet as a family and put His love into action. "Walk in love" urges a true imitation of Christ. It was because of His great love that He was willing to die on the cross.

Walk *circumspectly*
(EPHESIANS 5 V 15)

In other words carefully, prudently, decorously. Or, more plainly – we are to watch our step. In Colossians 4 v 5 we are urged to walk in wisdom and to "let your speech be always with grace, seasoned with salt, that ye may know how ye ought to answer every man." In so many ways Christians can be caught unawares. It matters very much how we conduct our lives. CF Andrews wrote in his book *What I Owe to Christ*: "The bloom of the rose does not need to proclaim itself loudly to the world. It's very perfume is the witness of its sweetness. So the Christian life that grows silently shedding its perfume on every side is the truest witness to Christ." We must be on our guard.

Walk *differently* :
"...walk henceforth not as other Gentiles walk,
in the vanity of their mind"
(EPHESIANS 4 V 17)

This does not mean that we have to keep ourselves apart. We want to live on good terms with our neighbours and friends, but we must agree to differ from those who do not share our Christian values and standards. We must be prepared to stand up for what we believe. When we open up our lives to Christ we become new people and because of the change cannot help but be noticed. We may often be caught up in circumstances where a stand has to be made and, by making that stand, being a means of others doing the same. We used to sing "Dare to be a Daniel, dare to stand alone; dare to have a purpose true, dare to make it known." We see many of the things we value slipping away and we feel very sad. But God's word is still the same and we have cause to rejoice that many Christians are seeking a greater commitment and are telling others of their changed lives. They are walking with Him in His way.

Let us be worthy of that vocation to which we have been called, and aim for(as William Cowper puts it) "a closer walk with God." Our hope is to be worthy of our calling – to walk in love, to walk carefully, to walk differently. Thank God that His grace is ever present to help us.

Stella Rowland

The Good Samaritan

(St. Luke 10 vv 25-37).

The road from Jerusalem to Jericho was a desolate stretch of about 23 miles, surrounded by scrub and desert, a road notoriously infested with bandits and thieves. On this road the Samaritan came across the poor man who had been robbed and left half dead. The story says that a Priest and a Levite looked and passed by but that the Samaritan saw and helped.

Here was a man *with his eyes open*. How we need to be like that. Often we are so preoccupied with our own selves that we fail to see the needs of others. Sometimes we see but, like the Priest and Levite, fail to act because we don't want to be involved. But what a difference when we see things for what they are. The lover of nature will stop and look at a flower or tree and will see hidden beauty that the passer by does not see. Again, how often we think we know all about someone we live with or is a close relative or friend and then they suddenly say or do something that surprises us. There were things we just hadn't noticed. The Priest and Levite both saw the man by the roadside but to them he was just something distressing. The Samaritan saw him in his need.

Jesus told this parable in answer to the question "Who is my neighbour?" So who is? Well, we don't have to look very far. "Lord God, open my eyes" is a prayer we need to pray every day. And what eye-openers there are. Surely no-one was as keen sighted as our Lord Himself. He saw the sometime wavering, sometime impulsive, Peter as a rock. He can see in the worst of us a new person.

The second thing about the Samaritan is that he was *open hearted.* We read that when he saw the poor man he was moved with compassion. Not only did he see but he was prepared to do something. How often do we find people who channel their emotions in the wrong way, who will go crazy about some "Star" or queue all night for tickets to see a famous performer yet can be unaware of real need that is close at hand. Jesus was filled with compassion. A woman caught in the very act of adultery was brought to Him and He refused to condemn her but urged her to sin no more. He spoke to a woman at a well in Samaria and led her to a new way of life. Like Jesus, the Samaritan saw and had compassion. He poured oil into the wounds, bound up the hurts, put the injured man on his donkey and brought him to an inn where he could be cared for.

Then we see that the Samaritan was *open handed*. He paid for the man's stay at the inn and promised that if there were further costs he would meet them when he came again. (Two pence in those days was equal to two day's wages.) We may see and even be moved by the sight of need but it is what we do about it that counts. The test of love is that it touches the pocket. In the lovely story about the woman anointing the feet of Jesus we learn that she didn't spare herself when she wanted to show her love. We all know that if we seek to follow in the steps of Jesus we must reckon with a costly demand. We can so easily lose heart trying, for instance, to love someone who is unloving. How wearing it is to try and show love when working with some folk who are destructive of it. But the only redemptive power in the world is inexhaustible love.

To be a genuine Good Samaritan is no small thing. It is easy to talk about it but not so easy to put it into effect. The Samaritan is but a reflection of Jesus and if we love it is because He first loved us. His life was a life of love in which He gave Himself for all mankind. In His own words: if we would follow Him we must be prepared to take up the cross. I cannot play my part if I do not feel the weight of that cross. The Samaritan reminds us always of Him who came not to be ministered to but to minister. Our Lord never shirked any responsibility that came His way. And today, just as in the days when He walked this earth, He knows our every need and no one is beyond the redemptive love of the Great Samaritan Himself.

The Women Who Followed Jesus

Women were the last at the cross and the first at the tomb. But who were those who followed Jesus, stood with Him in His agony and came to the tomb to give the last loving service they could to this man who meant so much to them?

Mary and Martha from Bethany had been friends of Jesus for a long time. In St. Luke 10 v 38 we see them in their home caring for Jesus. Martha is doing what she does so well – preparing and serving a meal. St. John 12 tells how Mary performs that wonderful act of anointing the feet of Jesus. Little did the two sisters realise that this would be the last time they would be able to minister to their friend. Their love for Jesus was never carefully eked out but given fully and generously. Real love doesn't count the cost.

One woman of whom we hear little but who tried to save Jesus from the cross was Pilate's wife. She had a dream that troubled her much. She knew, in her heart, that Jesus was innocent and sent a note to her husband telling him to have nothing to do with "that just man" (St. Matthew 27 v 19). She did her best but it wasn't enough to stop what was happening. I wonder what happened to her. Did she become a follower?

At the foot of the cross was Mary the mother of Jesus, Mary the wife of Cleophas and Mary Magdalene (St. John 19 v 25). We cannot enter into the feelings of our Lord's mother. From the beginning she knew her son was of God but she had to let Him go and do what He came into this world to do. But the anguish and pain she suffered must have been terrible. Then, in His last moments Jesus looked with love on her and committed her to his friend John's care. How, amidst her grief, her heart must have been warmed that this son of hers was concerned for her even in his own suffering.

Other women were at the cross (St. Matthew 27 vv 55, 56.) They had followed Jesus from Galilee. All we know of them is that they had ministered to Jesus – and they were at the cross. No need for names then, no need for telling us more about them – what they had done and where they were now was recorded and will live for ever. We don't even know in what capacity they ministered to the Lord. Providing food, doing the washing? Jesus and His disciples were in need of those things. The one thing we know is that they walked the roads with Him, ministering to Him and listening to His teaching.

Even when the apostles fled the cross the women were still there, they didn't desert their friend. So much loyalty and love is seen in this. They shared the most critical time. In St. Luke 23 v 55 we read :

> "And the women also which came with Him from
> Galilee followed after and beheld the sepulchre
> and how his body was laid."

Then they returned and prepared spices and rested on the Sabbath day. Right to the end we find them ministering to Jesus. It all reminds us so much of those who serve in a quiet way and perhaps are hardly noticed.

Then, St. Luke (chapter 24) says that very early in the morning they came bringing spices they had prepared – and found the tomb empty. John's description of that early morning is beautiful. He highlights Mary Magdalene who, when she found the tomb empty, ran to tell the disciples. I wonder – did they really believe her? However, they ran to see for themselves and then went home. But it was to Mary that Jesus revealed Himself. What joy for her –

"I have seen the Lord."

No doubting on her part, for Jesus had called her by name and as she had followed Him in obedience and loving service now she was called to go and tell the others. What a privilege was hers. She was the first to see the living Lord.

How joyful all those sorrowing women must have felt when they knew that their Lord was alive. Nor did they then go away. They and the disciples stayed together, meeting and praying and waiting for God's promise to send the Comforter to them. And the Comforter came. They had followed Jesus to the end and beyond that into a never-ending story. We look back at them in wonder and in love.

Things We Overhear

(St. Mark 5 vv 21-43)

We could spend ages talking about things we have overheard. Sometimes when out shopping, or in the bus queue, or at a meeting at Church, snippets of conversation come our way. We can, of course, get the wrong impression (what we have heard could prove to be dangerous and wrong if repeated) and so it is best forgotten (like the game we used to play in which we passed on whispers.)

In this chapter of St. Mark we have a lovely story about the raising of Jairus' daughter. Jairus, a ruler of the synagogue, came to Jesus because he was deeply troubled by his daughter's illness. (How often it takes trouble to bring us to Jesus.) But he came in faith for he said "Come and lay thy hands on her that she may be healed and she shall live."

So Jesus went with Jairus and the crowd followed. The woman with the issue of blood also came for healing. She too had to come in faith and went away healed. I wonder how Jairus felt all this time with the crowd and now this woman and all the while his child desperately ill? Did his faith waver a little when it seemed to him that Jesus was spending precious time with this woman in the crowd? Then at that critical moment there came someone from his house to tell him that he need not bother the teacher any further because the daughter was dead. Surely it must have passed through Jairus' mind to wonder why Jesus was so slow. If only he had made haste! It takes us back to the death of Lazarus and Martha's

"If you had been here my brother
would not have died."

We sometimes go through experiences when it seems that He is slow in coming to help or to answer our prayers. But He waits His time.

Jesus overheard the words spoken to Jairus and told the man not to fear, "only believe." Surely the messengers of the sad news were tactless? "No good bothering the teacher now – she's dead so what good can He do?" Poor Jairus, pulled between the two. "What more can be done? She's dead. Come back home and join those already mourning." And the man, Jesus, in whom he had put all the faith he could was saying "Be not afraid, only believe!" Who is he to listen to? To which word is he to give place in his heart: "Don't worry" or "She's dead."?

Meanwhile it seems that Jesus Himself took over the situation for He went on His way to the mourning household. There, the crying and wailing was no atmosphere in which He wished to work. "Stop this" he tells them, "she isn't dead but sleeping." At which they laughed at Him. Then He put them all out of the house. All this time Jairus was looking on, his faith sorely put to the test.

Jesus takes father and mother and Peter, James and John, into the room and the miracle was performed. And in all this we have to look at the faith of Jairus, for it would seem that it was the key to the whole matter. He could so well have told Jesus not to bother when he heard that his daughter was dead. But he took Jesus home and trusted His word – "only believe." Can we imagine that Jesus would go so far with Jairus, build up his hope, and then disappoint him? Surely they will never be ashamed who trust in God's word.

One last look at the faith of Jairus. It was not great and magnificent, really it was little and weak, for when he saw the miracle that that faith accomplished he was overcome with amazement. What a strange thing faith is, for even though it is weak and small it can at the same time be responsible for allowing Jesus Christ into situations in which He can do great things. Therein is the hope and assurance for us that God can take what weak faith we have and use it to His glory.

Hebrews 11 tells us that faith gives substance to our hopes and makes us certain of realities we do not yet see. I read somewhere that we should trust God even when we cannot see and rely upon Him when we cannot understand. Surely, such was the faith of Jairus.

As we look at our own lives, sometimes wondering how big or small our faith is, we must realise that that is not what matters. It is what we do with whatever faith we have that is important. The grain of mustard seed is tiny but if planted will grow. Will we trust ourselves, our cares, our burdens, our needs to Jesus? Are we prepared to trust this: that all things are possible to Him although they may seem impossible to us?

Trust

What a wonderful thing it is to have someone that you can trust implicitly. Someone you know will respect all your confidences. A friend you can always go to knowing that they are totally to be trusted: the same kind of trust that a child has for a loving parent; a child who, when filled with fear, will take hold Mum's or Dad's hand and all the fear goes because now they feel safe. There is a lovely verse in a hymn :

"As trustful as a child who looks up in his mother's face,
and all his little griefs and fears forgets in her embrace.
So I to Thee, my Saviour look and in Thy face divine,
Can read the love that will sustain as weak a faith as mine."

I think of a couplet from another hymn :

"By prayer let me wrestle and He will perform,
With Christ in the vessel I'll smile at the storm."

No need to be fearful, then, when we put our trust in Him. In our every day lives we need a great deal of faith and trust to see us through. So we come to Jesus, putting our trust in the One who never fails.

We ask for guidance, knowing full well that if we let Him lead all will be well. But so often we think we know best. Even when we ask for His way we then go our own. This is where we find trust so difficult. Especially do we find it difficult when we are going through bad times. To be able to leave it all to the Father, knowing that He knows our need doesn't come easily. In Daniel chapter 3 we get a wonderful instance of real trust. We know the story of Shadrach, Meshach and Abednego who answered the king: "If it be so, our God whom we serve, is able to deliver us from the burning furnace, and He will deliver us out of thine hand, O king." What trust those men had! "He is able and He will." And the Lord did not fail them, He brought them through that great tribulation and by their trust and faith the king believed also. What a wonderful result of trust that was.

Then, if we go to the 1st Book of Samuel, chapter 17, we read how David killed Goliath. With what assurance David spoke (v. 37): "The Lord, who delivered me from the paw of the lion and from the paw of the bear; He will deliver me from the hand of this Philistine." Goliath with sword and spear and David with a sling and a stone! Nothing is impossible to God. If we will accept the challenge He will equip us with the vital necessities. What trust David needed even to speak these words, but he did, indeed, trust God to give him the victory.

We all have to learn this lesson of implicit, utter trust, and when we begin to learn it then God is really able to help us. By learning to trust Him we learn to know Him more fully. Psalm 146 tells us: "Put not your trust in princes, nor in the son of man, in whom there is no help." Somewhere else I read "But trust in the Lord with all thy heart and lean not unto thine own understanding." Isaiah says "Thou wilt keep him in perfect peace whose mind is stayed on Thee, because he trusteth Thee." Jeremiah says: "Blessed is the man that trusteth in the Lord and whose hope the Lord is." We know from our daily lives how needful it is to trust one another in all our earthly enterprises. We have to take God on trust too if we are to progress in our spiritual life.

"Sing, pray, and swerve not from His ways,
But do thine own part faithfully;
Trust His rich promises of grace,
So shall they be fulfilled in thee:
God never yet forsook at need
The soul that trusted Him indeed."

(GEORG CHRISTIAN NEUMARK, 1621-81)

What A Woman!

(PROVERBS 31 VV 10-31).

What an amazing woman is described in this chapter! Solomon must have known much about women and here was his description of the ideal. What a list of virtues! She was always busy doing something for the good of her family – we cannot imagine her having even five minutes chat over the garden wall. And surely she would never have found time to go out. She was an early riser; she never minded how much trouble she took to give pleasure to her husband; she was a business woman; she made fine linen and sold it; she bought a field. Moreover there is that lovely touch in verse 21 which tells us that she was not afraid for her family when the snow came "for all her household are clothed in scarlet." In short, she did all that she could and then *simply gave up worrying.*

I am sure it would be very difficult to find such a woman today. How many of us worry about things that we cannot seem to help. And how many lives are blighted by fears which, again, we seem unable to escape – fear of things, of being shut in for instance, fear of heights, of pain or loss or death – or spiders or, oh, so many things. Mothers are often fearful, too, for their children. How we try to protect them, especially when epidemics are around. The story goes of the mother who was so fearful for her child that she always carried a thermometer in her handbag. The mother became worn out with worry that her child might catch something. Then one day she said to herself: "What am I afraid of? If anything happens to my child she is not beyond God's care." There are so many things that can endanger children outside as well as inside the home, and the only thing parents can do is as the woman in our reading: wrap them in the double garments of prayer and sound teaching in the home. Our anxieties we can take to God and leave with Him.

Sometimes we are afraid of what others will think of us. We are anxious to be well thought of, to look nice, to be admired. If we look at that clearly we see it to be pride. What a difference if, instead of thinking about what people would say, we thought of what Jesus would say of our actions; if, instead of other motives, our decisions were taken to please Him.

We have fears about the future. Our Lord told us to take no thought for the morrow, something which is very difficult for us. But many folk have taken it to heart and found that He never let them down. Dr. Barnardo was at his wits end as to how to keep his 200 orphans warm when winter set in. His wife put sheets of newspaper between the blankets on the beds but it didn't help much. The good Doctor told the Lord about it and the next morning there arrived a letter from a man who had heard of the situation and had despatched a bale of 200 blankets. God had taken care of it and met the need almost before the prayer was uttered.

We must not think, however, that this promise of God's care means that we shall never be hurt. Jesus doesn't promise an easy passage. We may well have to take up our cross, but we can be sure that nothing can snatch us out of His love. So we need not be afraid of the future – it is safe in His keeping and He will guide us through it. He will be our companion. The trouble is that we are so often too busy with trivial things to recognise His presence. If we recognise that presence (especially in our homes) we shall not be ruffled by the irritations that come our way. We shall know His peace in our hearts. He can turn our anxieties into confident hopes and grant us a peace which the world can but marvel at.

When Jesus Comes

(St. John 20)

At a time when the disciples were met together full of gloom, very sad and so troubled in their hearts – Jesus came amongst them. Although He had said He would rise from the dead, and although Mary Magdalene had said that she had seen the Lord, they were not sure. Then, as they met together, trying to console one another, suddenly the Lord Himself appeared in their midst. And what did He say?

"Peace be unto you."

One disciple, Thomas, was missing and when they told him what had happened he could not believe. But eight days afterwards they were all met together again and Jesus came. Again those words:

"Peace be unto you."

To have peace in one's heart is a wonderful thing. We live in a world where there seems to be little peace and little trust. There is so much tumult and anxiety. We so much need to pray daily for the peace of the world. But we can have peace within ourselves as we find it in Christ our Saviour. His peace is given "not as the world gives" so our hearts are to be neither troubled nor afraid. I think of times when our Lord used words of peace.

"Go in peace, you faith hath made you whole."
"Blessed be the peacemakers for
they shall be called the children of God."

"Peace be unto you."

Jesus came again when the disciples had been out all night fishing and caught nothing (John 21). As they drew into land a voice asked whether they had caught any fish. They did not recognise the Lord. "Put your nets on the other side" said the voice; so they did and they had that miraculous catch of fish, big fish. It was John who said to Peter, "It is the Lord." Then Jesus fed them having already prepared a meal of fish and bread. He invited them "Come and eat." Did they, I wonder, remember His words :

"He who eateth of the bread
that I give shall never hunger."

Do we, again I wonder, hold in our hearts His assurance that

"I am the bread of life."?

Just as we need food for our bodies we need spiritual food. It is so wonderful to think that Jesus offered food to the disciples. He knew their need. He did the menial task of preparing food for them. He offers to us day by day all that we need. A hymn says "All that I need is in Jesus" and goes on "Life would be worthless without Him, all things in Jesus I find." And so we do. We all need spiritual food day by day in order that we may grow in grace. He comes to us as He came to the disciples and He has prepared food for us.

Jesus comes very personally to Peter and says "Feed my sheep; feed my lambs." It is almost as though He is saying "As I have fed you so feed my sheep." Peter had made many blunders, especially when he denied that he knew Jesus. So this encounter must have been very wonderful to him. To think that Jesus loved him so much that He was giving him this great job to do – handing over to him His own appointed role as the Good Shepherd, to care for the young and the old, to feed them with the word of God. "I am the bread of life; whosoever eateth of this bread shall never hunger, and whosoever drinketh of the water that I shall give will never thirst." Peter was commissioned to this task – to proclaim God's loving provision for His people.

Jesus comes to dispirited and tired followers giving new life. There are two on the Emmaus road and the stranger they meet gives new strength and new hope. The roads to Damascus and Emmaus both represent ways in which Jesus can come and totally transform a situation and people's way of thinking. Once the two on the Emmaus road recognise Jesus they are new people, there is no delay in their eagerness to get back to Jerusalem and testify that they have seen the Lord. They are filled with new life. When Jesus comes and we let Him take possession He gives us new life. Isn't that just wonderful? Jesus comes with everlasting peace; He comes with spiritual food and as His word dwells in us we become new. How much we need that in order to grow in grace. He comes with new life and hope to the downhearted and beaten. How can we thank Him enough that He comes into the world and dies that we might have life eternal?

Jesus comes when we are busy
with our everyday lives;
He comes when we are
not expecting Him;
He may well come
unrecognised.

But He comes.
Praise God,
He comes!

A Spring Time Prayer

God grant this little springtime prayer
    And make our hearts, grown cold with care,
Once more aware of the waking earth
    Pregnant with life and the promise of birth.
For how can man have fear or doubt
    When on every side, all around and about,
The March winds blow across his face
    And whisper of God's power and grace?

Oh, give us faith to believe again
    That peace on earth, goodwill to men,
Will follow the "Winter of man's mind"
    And awaken his heart and make him kind.
And just as great Nature sends the Spring
    To give new birth to each sleeping thing,
God grant rebirth to man's slumbering soul
    And help him forsake his selfish goal.

A.E.R.